Travels
with
Thai Food

Travels
with
Thai Food

A Journey with Spirit House

Helen Brierty & Annette Fear

NEW HOLLAND

First published in Australia in 2007 by
New Holland Publishers (Australia) Pty Ltd
Sydney • Auckland • London • Cape Town

1/66 Gibbes Street Chatswood NSW 2067 Australia
218 Lake Road Northcote Auckland New Zealand
86 Edgware Road London W2 2EA United Kingdom
80 McKenzie Street Cape Town 8001 South Africa

Brierty, Helen.
Travels with Thai food : a journey with Spirit House.

Includes index.
ISBN 9781741105513 (pbk.).

1. Cookery, Thai. 2. Cookery - Thailand. 3. Food habits -
Thailand. 4. Tourism and gastronomy - Thailand. 5.
Thailand - Description and travel. I. Title.

641.59593

Publisher: Fiona Schultz
Project Editor: Lliane Clarke
Designer: Hayley Norman
Production: Linda Bottari
Printer: Tien Wah Press, Singapore

10 9 8 7 6 5 4 3 2 1

Acknowledgements

We have to thank our 'guinea pigs'—those first Tag-Along Tour participants who sipped and supped beyond the call of duty, over breakfast, lunch and dinner, with continuous snacking in between. All in the good cause of helping Spirit House chefs discover many of the taste sensations for this book.

When you're in a busy food market with no English signage, and you want to find something amazing, you need to stack the odds in your favour. You need people—about eight people with adventurous palates, a Spirit House chef and a guide who speaks Thai usually does the trick. Ten people, ten dishes and place your bets ... the chances of a new, delicious, unheard-of and unpronounceable dish coming up are much better than if you were on your own or travelling with a friend. This is definitely a situation where too many cooks can't spoil the broth!

All praise to Acland Brierty, our Tag-Along Guide—speaking rusty-fluent Thai learned while living in Bangkok during a misspent youth, his knowledge of street food, hidden alleys and food markets is what makes the tours such a success. Acland and his friend Anne Dowd's quick-on-the-draw camera skills resulted in these pages of incidental photographs and local colour images.

The majority of the recipes are contributed by Cooking School Head Chef, Annette Fear, a driving force behind its ten years of success. A veritable walking encyclopaedia of Asian ingredients and cooking methods, Annette's spare time is spent reading, cooking, tasting or growing Asian food.

Thank you also to our chefs, Kelly Lord and Katrina Ryan, for providing supplementary recipes and to all our staff, whose commitment to Spirit House ensures its success.

Contents

Introduction

In the midst of a cooking class at the Spirit House restaurant in 2005, chef Annette Fear mentioned she was going to Thailand to explore street food and regional specialties. One of the students commented she would love to tag along with her. The rest of the class all chorused 'we want to come too.' That simple aside remark led to the creation of Spirit House Tag-Along Tours to Thailand—and the writing of this book.

Like our tours, this book is a journey in Thai food. Part cookbook, part guide book, turn the pages and be taken on an exploration of Thai tastes, either in your home kitchen or out on the streets of Bangkok.

Most people's first encounter with Thai food is via their local Thai take-away. Walking the Bangkok streets puts Thai cuisine into context. Start pounding the hot pavements of Bangkok, and you quickly realise that the take-away Thai food we enjoy at home is just the tip of the chilli.

Bangkok streets are literally a smorgasbord, a veritable Thai banquet, of all that regional Thailand has to offer. This book helps to unlock the secrets of Thai ingredients, flavours and cooking methods.

There are descriptions of a variety of the more popular street food stalls, what is sold at each and what taste flavours you can expect when ordering from the ever smiling stall holders.

After devouring the contents, we guarantee you will decide never to eat in a tourist hotel again.

Included are maps and directions to several must-try Bangkok restaurants—home to a new breed of Thai chefs at the cutting edge of modern Thai cuisine. Kelly Lord has also featured some of the most popular modern Thai dishes from Spirit House restaurant menus—contemporary twists on this ancient exotic cuisine.

Call your friends for a dinner party, or call your travel agent for a flight to Bangkok. You're about to embark on a fantastic, taste-of-Thai adventure.

Thai cooking ingredients

Most large cities have Chinatowns where all the more exotic ingredients can be sourced from Asian supermarkets.

- **Thai basil:** quite distinctive aniseed taste, but can substitute with ordinary basil.
- **Kaffir lime leaves:** available frozen or fresh from supermarkets, don't use ordinary lime leaves.
- **Golden/Red shallots:** the Asian onion, substitute with red or brown onion. Looks just like a knob of garlic. Are also sliced then deep fried to make crispy fried shallots available in packets in Asian stores. Substitute with red onion, but not with green shallots, scallions or spring onions.
- **Krachai:** a ginger with an earthy, musky flavour. Buy pickled in jars.
- **Tamarind:** the pulp from seed pods of the tamarind tree. To make tamarind water, use one tablespoon of paste to ½ cup hot water. When softened push through sieve.
- **Pickled garlic:** available in jars in Asian supermarkets.
- **Galangal:** a member of the ginger family. Buy fresh or pickled in jars.
- **Palm sugar:** made from variety of palms including coconut, buy in rolls or jars. Colour indicates flavour—from creamy sweet to dark and smoky.
- **Dried shrimp:** used as a flavouring agent, buy in packets from Asian supermarkets.
- **Chillies:** range in heat from mild to wild. Adjust to suit personal taste.
- **Yellow bean sauce:** made from soya beans, buy in bottles in supermarkets.
- **Thai chilli paste with soya bean oil:** buy in jars in Asian supermarkets.
- **Sweet soy sauce:** sweetened with dark palm sugar. Best known by its Indonesian name, 'ketcap manis'.

A taste of Old Bangkok

here be dragons

Democracy Monument

Chu Tin: Famous for its dessert powders and self-serve Sa Rim, a refreshing dessert to end your tour of the old city.

Duck restaurants with air con rooms plus famous vegetarian restaurants. Look for the old lady selling traditional sweets.

Dinso Rd

Wat Mahan

Tiger Shrine

seaweed jelly drinks

Ci. Ha.

K. Tor M. Sq.

.a Meid: has been making om beuang pancakes for e than 50 years.

Kow Pa Nit: Famous for sticky rice and coconut cream. Mango vendors in front of shop.

Amazing temple supply shops and small factories casting huge bronze buddhas.

Phrang Phuton

Chote Chitr Restaurant

Giant S

Wat Suth

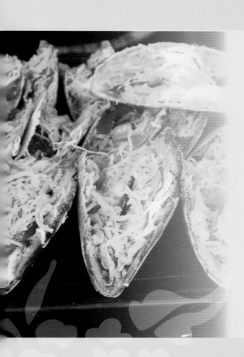

The 'Old City'—the original city of Bangkok—is a great place to explore and eat. Surrounded by thick fortified walls that are still preserved in places, there are specialty food stalls and restaurants that have been trading from old shops or houses for generations—the recipes passed on from mother to daughter through the years.

The streets are filled with shops selling huge Buddha figures, temple bells and other religious items for local temples. We befriended a charming lady who makes traditional candy from recipes that are hundreds of years old—an amazing blend of flavours and textures. There is a tiny 70-year-old restaurant that specialises in duck that has an air-conditioned room—welcome relief from the midday heat of the pavements.

A walk around the Old City gives you a real taste of Thailand.

Start at the Democracy Monument and walk down Dinso Road. As you make your way down the street to City Hall, you will pass specialty vegetarian restaurants. Directly opposite City Hall are some large duck restaurants with extensive menus (many in English) and air-conditioned rooms.

During the week you will find a delightful old lady selling traditional desserts on the street outside ... grab a bag or two and keep walking down the road.

Just before the road turns to the right, you will see a Brahmin shrine. Even though Thais are Buddhist, Brahmins are responsible for the main royal ceremonies and this temple is home to seven remaining Brahmin priests in Thailand.

Diagonally opposite the Brahmin shrine, is a giant red swing. The swing is over 200 years old and was used in a Brahmin ceremony to thank the gods for good crops. Teams of four men would swing on a log high in the air to grab a bag of coins suspended on a high pole, but many lost their lives and the ceremony was banned. If you visit Wat Suthat, you can see photos of the swing and explore this amazing temple, with hardly a tourist in sight.

As you turn the corner, notice the change in architecture with shop/houses making and decorating huge brass Buddha figures. This area was Bangkok's first 'shopping mall', built in the 1850s. The artisans in the area descend from bronze workers who were famous for making bronze look like gold. A walk down the laneways and into the shops reveals a treasure of sight and sound.

These Buddha stores can be much larger than they look, so find your way back to the main street and keep walking. The footpath has been taken over by the road, so be careful. You will come to a small round intersection, keep going straight ahead and then take the next lane to the right.

You are now in Phrang Phuton—an old palace that now comprises 140 combination shop/houses all renovated to their original glory and home to a tiny hole-in-the-wall restaurant called Chote Chitr which is world famous for mee grop, banana blossom salad and tom yum soup.

Exit Phrang Phuton through the lane on the right. When you hit the main street, you will see people selling mangos across the road. You have now found Kow Pa Nit—Thailand's most famous sticky rice and coconut milk shop. Cross the road and buy a mango from one of the vendors and a bag of the best sticky rice and coconut milk you will ever taste. Eat your mangos in Phrang Phuton or keep walking up the main road then take the next road on the left.

About 50 metres on the right side of this street is Mae La Meid, a small shop selling 'khanom beuang'—it has been in business for 50 or more years. Khanom Beuang is a simple crispy pancake made from soya flour with a coconut milk custard and a choice of three different toppings: pickled persimmon, sweet egg-yolk strands and prawns (shrimps) with white pepper. These tasty snacks are cooked to order, a fascinating process to watch and even better to eat.

Cross the road and buy a bag of the best sticky rice and coconut milk you will ever taste.

Head back to the main street and cross the road. Turn left and walk up the road, passing shops selling Thai donuts and refreshing jelly health drinks made from seaweed.

There is an interesting Chinese temple on the left and further on is a lovely Thai temple called Wat Mahan, a restful place to enjoy your Khanom Beuang. Back out on the street, keep walking until you come to the second last street on the right before you hit the major road ahead. Turn left and you've reached Chu Tin.

Chu Tin sells dessert powders and is famous for Sa Rin—fine angelic strands of agar agar served with a sweet syrup and ice. You simply serve yourself—take a bowl of multicoloured agar agar from the cabinet, add some ice and pour over the syrup—a great way to end your walk.

Head back out onto the main street and to the four lane road at the end of the street. From here you can catch a cab to the Grand Palace, only a kilometre away.

Street of Buddhas

A visit to Klong Thoey Market in Bangkok is an ideal place for lunch. This is the biggest fruit and vegetable market in Bangkok and features countless vendors selling exotic fresh ingredients. There is also an open-air fish and meat market that is not for weak stomachs but is fascinating to wander through. Lunch at the food stalls in this market means choosing from rows upon rows of traditional stalls selling everything from curries, soups, noodles, desserts, or local favourites.

In front of the Bangkok City Hall (see map on page 12) is a large square that is used occasionally for dances and ceremonies, but is mostly empty. In the past, it was a thriving market place and the area was famous for artisans who could make brass look like gold.

After the market was moved, local artists set up shop in the streets and hidden laneways diagonally opposite the temple. A short walk down one of these streets and you pass factories putting the final touches to a vast range of brass Buddhas, deities and temple bells.

Shops in this area are famous for selling essential monk offerings—monks' bowls, robes, umbrellas and candles. Traditionally, monks were not allowed to handle money or ask for supplies, so the temples rely on donations from devout followers to supply their daily needs. This is why you will see hundreds of plastic buckets filled with items like toothpaste, candles, robes, aspirin and detergent ready for people to buy, which they then donate to the temple or present to the monks when they perform family ceremonies.

This area is a treasure trove for anything related to Buddhist practice. Ceremonial tables and plinths are found here. Ornately carved cabinets for housing precious relics, temple bells, five-foot high candles, incense, temple umbrellas and fans are just the tip of the iceberg. Many of the homes in this area house small factories where the families manufacture these religious artifacts.

Food
on the street

Most Thai food is cooked on demand and in all our years of travelling through Thailand we have never been ill. Always look for vendors who store their ingredients on ice and avoid eating food that has been sitting out in the open.

What is amazing is just how many different dishes a small stall with one wok can produce. Ordering can be as simple as pointing at a dish another customer is eating and holding up one finger to signal you want one 'mystery' dish. The best thing is to have a group of friends with you and play Russian roulette: order three or four different items and share.

Som Tum

Jammed between two parked cars is a vendor selling barbecue chicken and 'som tum', green pawpaw (papaya) salad. Half an oil drum on the front makes a neat barbecue. But how would you know he sells som tum?

When you see the shredded pawpaw, tomatoes and limes in a glass cabinet it's a dead give-away for a som tum stall.

Once you have found a barbecue of roasting chicken, or a vendor with a pile of shredded green pawpaw (papaya), you are ready to order. 'Kor … noi' means 'can I have … please? Simply say: ' Kor som tum noi' which translates as 'can I have some som tum please?' Unless you've learned to count in Thai, just hold up one or more fingers to indicate how many dishes you'd like. To buy some barbecue chicken say: 'Kor gai yarng noi'.

Add to your dish a Thai salad or 'yum' which comes in many flavours and variations. You can order strips of green mango served with a pungent sauce of shrimp paste, palm sugar, chilli and fish sauce plus a bag of chilli powder, sugar and salt.

In the ice coolers on most of these stalls is 'khow neeo'—sticky rice—great to go with your barbecue chicken and som tum. Once you've ordered, take a seat and the vendor will bring the food to you. Payment is when you've finished your meal.

If you want take away, just ask them to: 'Sai toong noi' which means 'put it in a plastic bag.'

Noodles

Noodle vendors are easy to spot, just look for metal carts with stacks of noodles behind a glass window. Commonly known as 'gwoy teeo' in Thai, you simply point at the sort of noodle you want and then choose your meat, most commonly a fish ball or dumpling.

Because 'gwoy teeo' is a Chinese dish, you eat these with chopsticks. On the table you will find small bowls of sugar, fish sauce, vinegar and chilli powder—add these to your noodle bowl to adjust the flavours.

Meat

As you walk the streets of Bangkok you find small carts with duck or pork hanging in the small display window. These carts supply a simple meal of meat and rice often with a rich gravy ladled over the top.

If you find some roast ducks—or 'bpet yarng' in Thai—hanging in a shop window or on a stall, in a few minutes you will have a delicious dish of roast duck on rice with a special sauce. In the middle of the table you will find some sweet soya sauce with a few chillies in it ... add that to your 'bpet yarng'.

Thais love their pork and when you see strips of red pork hanging in a window, you're in for a treat. Often served with special gravy, these stalls are identifiable by large pork hocks sitting in a pot of simmering stock or strips of red pork hanging in the window. If you're tired of pointing and ordering you can order in Thai by saying: 'khaa moo' for leg of pork, 'moo dang' for roasted red pork and 'moo grob' is crispy pork ... all delicious.

Rice

Another commonly found street vendor serves dishes with rice as the base—fried rice with pork or chicken, omelettes, diced pork and basil or a delicious noodle dish called 'pat si yoo'. All these can usually be found at roadside vendors who have eggs, flat noodles and leafy vegetables displayed in the window of their stand.

The best way to find out if you have the right vendor is to ask: 'Mee khow pat my?' meaning, 'do you have fried rice ('khow pat')?' If they have, they will reply 'mee'. If not—'my mee'. Asking this is much easier than learning how to read Thai.

Try Thai style fried rice by saying: 'kor khow pat moo (pork) or gai (chicken) noi'. Adjust the flavour of the fried rice by spooning from the bowl of fish sauce with chillies that is always set on each table.

There is also a vast cornucopia of pre-cooked food displayed from which you can choose. Once again, these will be served with rice. Although eating this sort of food isn't as safe as eating something that is freshly cooked, there are some amazing dishes to try at these street stalls. You can usually judge the quality of the food by the number of Thai people eating at a stall.

Drinks
[Deum]
& drinking food
[kap klem]

Thailand's huge variety of tropical fruits makes it a juice paradise. Fresh orange juice vendors are everywhere on Bangkok streets. These oranges resemble small limes and are sweet like a mandarin. Many tourists mistakenly think sugar has been added, but Thai vendors would usually add salt to a drink before they would think of adding sugar.

Nearly as popular as orange juice is fresh sugar cane juice. Keep an eye out on the streets for sugar cane crushers which look like your grandmother's old washing mangle (for younger readers ..... just Google it!) You'll often find sugar cane juice in plastic bottles, slightly yellow in colour.

Coconut juice is so popular that there are factories devoted to shaping the tops, making it easy for the street vendor to cut open and add the drinking straw.

Iced drinks

Apart from serving Thai tea or 'sock' coffee, drink vendors also offer iced tea, coffee, and a bizarre range of iced syrups. Popular with Thais is a pandanus cordial—just point to the bright green bottle and make the symbol for one, and there's your sugar fix for the day.

Cordials are a very common street drink, with the most popular flavours being pandanus, coconut and raspberry. Just ask the vendor to 'sai toong' which means to put it in a bag. The bag is then closed with a rubber band and a straw inserted. It's a perfect way to carry your drink around the markets with the added advantage of being able to hang it on the handlebars of your motorbike—if you happen to be crazy enough to ride a motorbike in Bangkok

A unique tea, served both hot or cold and sweetened with sugar and condensed milk is cha Thai—it gets its orange colour from an infusion of ground tamarind seeds.

Singha Beer is the favourite lager beer of the Thais. Based on an original Danish recipe introduced at the turn of the century, it has a unique flavour that makes it a perfect accompaniment to Thai food.

More affordable than beer, rice whiskeys are distilled from sticky rice, the most famous brand being Mekong. A common sight in restaurants is a small shelved table at the end of each dining table, holding whiskey, ice, mixes like Coke or soda water, and sometimes limes. This is because Thai whiskey is rarely drunk neat. Usually a teenager attends the table, mixing the drinks and continually topping them up. This leaves your table free for more food—and is a powerful way to get drunk!

A chilled glass of Mekong, ice and water with a squeeze of lime goes perfectly with 'yum' salads.

Drinking food

In Thailand, having a drink usually includes enjoying 'drinking food', or kap klaem. From a simple bowl of cashews fried together with garlic, Kaffir lime, salt and ginger through to dried beef or a spicy 'miang', there is quite a range of drinking food available on the Bangkok streets.

Sweet Pork & Peanut Dip

This simple dip is great with a cassava cracker and the first drink of the night.

1 teaspoon coriander (cilantro) roots, peeled and chopped
1 tablespoon garlic, chopped
2 tablespoons vegetable oil
1 teaspoon roasted chilli paste
100g (3½oz) pork mince
1 tablespoon golden shallots, peeled and sliced
2 tablespoons palm sugar
1 tablespoon fish sauce
150 ml (5fl oz) coconut milk
1 tablespoon peanuts, roasted and ground

Pound coriander (cilantro) root and garlic in a mortar and pestle until fine.

Remove paste from mortar and fry gently in a heavy-based pot with vegetable oil and chilli paste.

Add pork mince and shallots and fry until golden.

Add sugar and fish sauce and coconut milk a little at a time to prevent sauce from splitting.

Stir through peanuts and set aside to cool.

Serve with prawn crackers or sticks of fresh vegetables.

SERVES 4

Sweet Corn & Prawn Fritters

Simple to make—all the family will love these.

500g (1lb) green prawn (shrimps)
roughly chopped
2 tablespoons red curry paste
2 tablespoons fish sauce
2 tablespoons cornflour
1 egg, beaten
¼ cup finely sliced spring onions
½ cup fresh or frozen cooked
corn kernels

In a food processor, mince prawns (shrimps) to a paste. Add red curry paste, fish sauce, cornflour and egg. Combine well.

Put into a bowl, mix in onions and corn kernels. Wet hands and shape into flat round cakes. Deep fry in vegetable oil until fritters are golden brown. Drain on kitchen paper.

Serve with Cucumber Relish (page 70) and Sweet Chilli Dipping Sauce (page 180).

SERVES 4-6

Red Pork

Red pork can be found all over Thailand in barbecue shops that also sell duck and chicken. The pork is often eaten as a snack with a drink, or cooked in a variety of ways with rice or noodles. The meat keeps well for a few days refrigerated, or can be frozen for later use.

½ teaspoon red food colouring diluted with water (optional)
1 pork neck cut into 4 pieces length ways
2 tablespoons Hoisin sauce
2 tablespoons Chinese rice wine
1 tablespoon light soy sauce
1 tablespoon dark soy sauce
3 cloves garlic, crushed
1 tablespoon ginger, chopped
3 star anise, crushed coarsely
1 tablespoon sesame oil
1 tablespoon sugar
1 tablespoon fish sauce
2 tablespoons honey

If using the food colouring, rub it well into the pork pieces while wearing rubber gloves. Combine the remaining ingredients, except for the honey, in a glass dish. Add the pork covering well with the marinade and refrigerate, covered, overnight.

Preheat oven to 180°C (350°F, moderate, gas mark 4).

Place on a rack in a large baking pan and add enough water to come just below the rack. Remove the pork from the marinade and add the honey to the reserved marinade. Place pork on cake rack, cook for 1 hour basting often with the reserved marinade. Remove from oven and rest for 15 minutes before slicing.

SERVES 6-8

Heavenly Beef

Deep fried sugar coated beef will certainly not get the Heart Foundation tick of approval. But just a little can be very satisfying, especially when eaten Thai style with a cold beer.

3 cups (750ml, 24fl oz) vegetable oil
500g (1lb) rump steak, cut into
5 x 2cm (2 x ¾ inch) strips
3 tablespoons light palm sugar
2 tablespoons fish sauce
2 teaspoons freshly ground white pepper

Heat oil in wok to medium. Cook the steak in batches until dark brown, about 3-4 minutes.

Drain on paper towel.

In a clean wok combine the palm sugar and fish sauce, bring to the boil and simmer until the sugar is dissolved. Add the beef and stir-fry until the meat is coated with the sauce. Stir in pepper.

Transfer to platter and serve at room temperature.

SERVES 4–6

Grilled Beef

This simple dish from the north is known as 'crying tiger'—a reference to the heat of the sauce. A good dish for the macho chilli eaters who like to say 'make it as hot as you can.'

250g (½lb) piece of rump steak
1 tablespoon oyster sauce

Sauce:
6 tablespoons lime juice
4 tablespoons fish sauce
1 teaspoon white sugar
1 teaspoon roasted chilli powder
2-6 small Thai birds eye chillies, finely sliced
1 golden shallot, sliced
2 tablespoons chopped coriander (cilantro) leaves
1 teaspoon roasted rice powder

To make sauce: combine all ingredients in a bowl.

Rub meat with the oyster sauce and barbecue on high for about 5-7 minutes each side for about medium rare. Remove from heat and transfer to a plate, cover loosely with foil and rest for about 10-15 minutes before slicing. Transfer to a platter and serve with the sauce on the side.

SERVES 4-6 WITH DRINKS, OR 1 BIG BLOKE WITH BEER

Rice
[Khao]

In Thailand, eating is a communal activity—a large number of diners offer a great choice of dishes. The ideal meal is a harmonious blend of spicy, hot, and sweet and sour flavours, and offers a variety of textures, from crispy and crunchy to creamy and wet. The meal should appeal not just to the palate, but also to the eyes and nose. A good Thai meal is a treat for all the senses.

But at all Thai meals, the bowl of rice is the centrepiece—other dishes on the table are mere accompaniments to the rice.

Spoon a mound of rice on to your plate, add small portions of the other dishes to the side and savour the contrasting textures and flavours.

Fragrant, long grain jasmine scented rice is the classic Thai rice, one of the best quality rice varieties in the world. Jasmine rice can be boiled, steamed, or re-heated by frying. It is used to make rice vinegars, soothing soups and is ground into flour for baking rice cakes. Cheap and nutritious, jasmine rice is practically the perfect foodstuff.

Sticky rice can't be stirred like jasmine rice, the glutinous ball must be tossed round and round to ensure even cooking, preferably in a basket over a charcoal burner. The shape of the woven basket allows the vendor to 'toss' the rice without burning their hands or spilling the sticky rice. A charcoal burner maintains a constant heat and cleans up some wood scraps as well. Sticky rice is commonly used to make rice-based desserts and cakes.

Chinatown

Chinatown, in the heart of Bangkok, is an amazing blend of sights, sounds and culture. Grab a map, take the ferry to any of the piers near Chinatown and just wander around the markets, laneways, alleys and streets—you will be overwhelmed by everything that's on offer.

Sticky Rice

This short grain rice is the staple of northern Thailand, where it is rolled into a ball with the fingers and used to scoop up the other food on the table.

2 cups sticky rice
water

Cover sticky rice with cold water and soak overnight.

Drain and steam over boiling water for approximately 30-40 minutes in steamer basket lined with clean cloth or muslin.

SERVES 4-6

Coconut Rice

This rice goes very well with spicy curries or 'yam' salads.

1 ½ cups of jasmine rice
400 ml (14fl oz) can of coconut milk
½ cup (125ml, 4fl oz) water
1 teaspoon white sugar
pinch of salt

Rinse the rice several times to remove the starch.

Put the coconut milk, water, salt and sugar into a large saucepan. Stir until the sugar is dissolved and the mixture is well blended.

Add the rice and steam for 20-25 minutes.

SERVES 4

Thai Fried Rice with Chicken

This most popular street food dish is Thai fast food at its best! Always prepared from cold, cooked rice, fried rice is a way of using up leftover rice from dinner the night before. When in Thailand, forgo your hotel breakfast with its predictable eggs and bacon. Ask hotel staff for directions to the nearest fried rice vendor and give your taste buds their first treat of the day!

4 tablespoons vegetable oil

2 eggs, beaten

1 red onion, diced

250g (8oz) chicken meat, chopped

4 cups cold, cooked jasmine rice

1 tablespoon fish sauce

1 tablespoon of palm sugar

1 tomato, cut into thin wedges

3 spring onions, sliced

2 cups bean sprouts

2 tablespoons crushed, roasted, unsalted peanuts

coriander (cilantro) leaves

1 tablespoon soy sauce

SERVES 4

To cook fried rice

Place one tablespoon of oil in a wok over medium heat, add the egg and scramble it. Set aside.

Add remaining oil to wok. When hot, add the onion, chicken and Garlic Coriander Pepper Paste.

Stir-fry until chicken is almost cooked. Add rice, fish sauce, soy sauce, sugar and stir-fry for one minute.

Add tomato and scrambled egg and stir-fry for one minute. Transfer to serving platter, garnish with spring onions, bean sprouts and peanuts.

Serve with a side dish of Hot and Sour Sauce.

Garlic Coriander Pepper Paste

A simple, extremely useful paste, these three ingredients are the most important combinations of aromatics and spices in Thai cuisine. Used sometimes to simply season a dish, and at others as the basis of a more complex paste.
Make fresh as required.

(MAKES 1/4 CUP)
½ teaspoon whole white peppercorns
1 tablespoon chopped coriander (cilantro) root and stem
8 cloves peeled and chopped garlic

Pound white peppercorns in mortar and pestle. Add coriander (cilantro) and garlic and pound to a paste.

Hot and Sour Sauce

Classic red chilli sauce that can be used for a dipping sauce or as a salad dressing. Leave sauce for 15 minutes before using to allow the flavours to merge.

4 red chillies
2 cloves garlic, chopped
1 onion, chopped
4 tablespoons fish sauce to taste
8 tablespoons fresh lime juice
4 teaspoons palm sugar to taste

Pound chopped chillies and garlic together until forming paste texture. Transfer to a bowl, add chopped onion, fish sauce, lime juice and sugar to taste. Stir well to mix. Adjust flavours so that sauce is equally salty and sour with a touch of sweetness.

Golden or red shallots: available in Asian supermarkets and used throughout Thai cuisine. You can substitute with brown or red onion.

Steamed Rice Dumplings Stuffed with Pork & Peanuts

An easy version of a popular Thai street food snack.

Filling:

4 cloves garlic

¼ cup chopped coriander (cilantro) root

½ teaspoon white peppercorns

3 tablespoons fish sauce

2 tablespoons light palm sugar

250g (8oz) pork mince

24 small dry rice papers

soft lettuce leaves

½ cup coriander (cilantro) leaves to garnish

½ cup coarsely crushed roasted peanuts

red vinegar to dip

Make a paste with the garlic, coriander (cilantro) and white pepper.

In a bowl, dissolve the palm sugar in the fish sauce and then add the pork mince and the paste. Mix together.

Soak the rice papers in a bowl of warm water until just softened. Place a teaspoon of the pork filling in the centre and fold into a package. Steam in a bamboo steamer over a wok half full of water for about 7 minutes.

Serve on a platter with the lettuce leaves, coriander (cilantro) leaves and peanuts. The dumplings are wrapped in the lettuce along with the coriander (cilantro) and peanuts.

Serve the red vinegar as a side dish.

SERVES 6-8

Spiced Saffron Rice

A rice dish like this is often served on special festive occasions.

4 cloves of garlic, peeled

2.5cm (1 inch) piece of ginger, peeled and chopped

5 tablespoons ghee or butter

4 golden shallots (or ½ cup onion), peeled and finely sliced

1 cinnamon stick

3 whole cloves

3 cardamom pods

2 star anise

3 cups long grain rice, rinsed and drained

5 cups (1.25l, 40fl oz) water

½ cup (125 ml, 4fl oz) coconut cream

½ teaspoon saffron threads soaked in hot water

crispy shallots to garnish

Pound the garlic and ginger to a paste in a mortar and pestle. Heat the butter in a large heavy based saucepan and fry the paste, shallots, and spices until fragrant. Add the drained rice and stir until well coated with the spice mix. Add the water, coconut cream and saffron water. Bring to the boil stirring gently. Then reduce to a very low heat and cover. Cook until the rice has absorbed all the water. This takes about 20 minutes. Transfer to a serving platter and garnish with the crispy shallots.

SERVES 6

Thai Style Pineapple
Fried Rice with Pork & Crab

A Spirit House variation of the classic Thai fried rice. Present this rice dish in a pineapple shell for special occasions.

1 pineapple, halved. Remove flesh and chop roughly to produce 150g (5oz)

2 tablespoons vegetable oil

4 golden shallots (or ½ cup onion) sliced

6 cloves garlic, chopped

200g (7oz) pork fillet, finely chopped

2 teaspoons curry powder

1 tablespoon palm sugar

2 tablespoons fish sauce

1 tablespoon soy sauce

4 cups cold cooked jasmine rice

125g (4oz) crab meat

2 tablespoons roasted cashews

½ cup coriander (cilantro) leaves

2 green shallots, sliced

1 red chilli, sliced

Cut the pineapple in half lengthways and remove the flesh from both halves. Chop finely.

Heat the oil in a wok. Add the shallots and garlic and cook for a few minutes.

Add the pork and stir-fry until brown.

Add the curry powder, palm sugar, fish sauce, soy sauce and stir until combined.

Add the rice and stir-fry until heated through.

Add the crab, cashews and pineapple. Spoon into the pineapple shells and garnish with coriander (cilantro) leaves, shallots and chilli strips.

SERVES 4

Eggs

[Khai]

Preserved, boiled, scrambled, simmered ...

Eggs play such an important part in the daily diet, not just in Thailand, but all across Asia. Since most rural houses raise hens and ducks, eggs are readily available and provide a cheap reliable source of protein. Just as in the West, eggs are used in a multitude of ways.

Eggs are preserved by salting then storing in tightly lidded earthenware jars. A fried egg is often the finishing flourish on top of a bowl of fried rice, while thin omelettes are used as wrappers, or shredded and tossed through stir-fry noodle dishes.

Hard-boiled eggs are added to salads or used to create unusual dishes such as 'son-in-law eggs' with its tamarind based sauce.

Eggs are scrambled, or turned into spicy omelettes with the addition of thin slithers of chicken or pork, herbs and chillies.

Beaten eggs are drizzled into simmering broth soups, or trailed from finger tips into a hot oiled pan to make beautifully lacy egg nets—the creative ways to utilise a simple egg appear endless.

Duck eggs are frequently used in Thai desserts because of their stronger flavour and albumen structure that makes for lighter steamed cakes, so popular at street food stalls.

SAFFRON ROBES

One of the most expensive spices in the world, saffron is also a powerful dye. It takes the stamens of 50,000 saffron crocus flowers to make half a kilogram of the dried spice.

Saffron flowers need to be harvested quickly, as they flower and wilt in the same day and the plants only bloom for a week or two. Even in small quantities, a few stamens are enough to impart a luminous yellow colour to cloth.

Traditionally, saffron coloured cloth was worn exclusively by Indian noble and high classes—probably because they were the only people who could afford it. As a result, saffron became associated with nobility and respect, which is why Buddhist monks wear saffron robes to this day.

Steamed Eggs with Pork & Ginger

A creamy savoury custard that is served as a cooling accompaniment to fiery curries and relishes

125g (4oz) minced pork
1 teaspoon finely chopped ginger
1 tablespoon fish sauce
white pepper to season
3 eggs
½ cup (125ml, 4fl oz) chicken stock or water
2 green shallots, finely chopped
coriander (cilantro) leaves to garnish

Place the pork, ginger, fish sauce and pepper in a bowl. Whisk the eggs and stock together and add to the pork. Add the shallots and stir to combine. Divide between heatproof cups or ramekins. Place in a bamboo steamer basket and steam over a gentle heat for 15-20 minutes or until the custard has set. Remove ramekins from steamer basket and garnish with coriander (cilantro) leaves

SERVES 4-6

Duck Egg Salad with Young Ginger

This salad is served in restaurants throughout Thailand and traditionally uses 'thousand year old eggs'. These Chinese preserved duck eggs are rather an acquired taste for the Western palate. We suggest using fresh duck or chicken eggs.

4 duck or 6 chicken eggs

1 small Cos lettuce

1 cup young ginger, peeled and finely shredded

1-2 medium hot red chillies, finely sliced

1 cup green shallots (spring onions, scallion), sliced

2 golden shallots, peeled and finely sliced

¾ cup (185ml, 6fl oz) lime juice

¼ cup (60ml, 2fl oz) fish sauce

1-2 tablespoons light palm sugar

coriander (cilantro) sprigs to garnish

Bring a large pot of water to boil and carefully place in eggs, reduce heat and cook 10 minutes for duck eggs or 5-6 minutes for chicken eggs. Remove when ready with slotted spoon and place in a bowl of cold water and set aside.

Clean the lettuce, reserving the large outer leaves and shred the heart.

Peel the eggs and cut into quarters lengthways and then in half crossways. Place the eggs in a bowl with the ginger, chillies, green shallots and golden shallots.

In a separate bowl combine the lime juice, fish sauce and palm sugar. Stir to dissolve the sugar. Add the dressing to the egg salad and mix to combine.

Line a serving plate with the large lettuce leaves and then make a bed with the shredded lettuce. Transfer the egg salad to the lettuce and garnish with the coriander (cilantro).

SERVES 6-9 AS PART OF A SHARED MEAL

Barbecue Pork Omelette with Tomato & Ginger Sauce

The oil in the wok needs to be smoking hot to create this puffed and golden omelette.

250g (1lb) pork neck

For the marinade:

1 tablespoon fermented red bean curd

1 tablespoon light soy sauce

1 tablespoon Chinese rice wine

½ tablespoon yellow bean sauce

1 tablespoon Hoisin sauce

1 tablespoon castor sugar

1 garlic clove, minced

To finish:

2 tablespoons honey

Tomato Ginger Sauce:

¼ cup (60ml, 2fl oz) peanut oil

2 tablespoons ginger finely chopped

2 garlic cloves finely chopped

2 tomatoes cut into thin wedges

1 teaspoon salt

1 teaspoon white sugar

1 tablespoon Chinese rice wine

½ cup (125ml, 4fl oz)chicken stock or water

1 tablespoon oyster sauce

For each omelette:

4 large eggs

¼ cup green shallots (spring onions, scallion), thinly sliced

1 teaspoon fish sauce

1 teaspoon pickled cabbage, finely chopped

1 tablespoon water

¼ cup (60ml, 2fl oz) vegetable oil

50g (1½oz) bean sprouts

Cut the pork neck into strips to resemble loins. Combine the marinade ingredients and pour over the pork. Marinate overnight if possible.

Preheat the oven to 240°C (500°F, very hot, gas mark 7). Fill a baking dish with water and cover with a cake rack. Place the pork strips on the rack (they should be suspended over the water) and roast for 45 minutes.

Reserve the marinade for the sauce. Heat the honey and brush over the pork strips. Cool and then slice thinly.

Make the Tomato Ginger Sauce: heat the oil in a wok and fry the ginger and garlic till fragrant.

Add the tomatoes, salt, sugar and Chinese rice wine. Fry till the tomatoes are soft then add the chicken stock and oyster sauce.

Bring to the boil and remove from the heat. Keep warm.

Make the omelettes: Whisk the eggs with the fish sauce, pickled cabbage and water.

Heat the oil in a wok until very hot. Pour in the egg mixture and push the omelette into the centre as it cooks, tipping the runny uncooked egg to the outside.

Reduce the heat to low and put the bean sprouts and some slices of pork into the omelette. Fold the omelette over and tip off any excess oil if necessary, then slide it onto a plate.

Top with more pork, the rest of the shallots and a generous amount of Tomato Ginger Sauce.

SERVES 4

Scrambled Eggs with Prawns & Cucumber

A simple dish that can be eaten for lunch with rice or sometimes it's matched with a spicy curry. Delicious served with pork or chicken.

2 tablespoons vegetable oil
4 cloves garlic, crushed
300g (10oz) green prawns (shrimps)
1 tablespoon oyster sauce
1 tablespoon fish sauce
2 teaspoons light palm sugar
1 cucumber cut into
a 2cm (1inch) dice
large pinch ground white pepper
4 eggs, lightly beaten
handful coriander (cilantro) leaves

Heat oil in wok to medium. Add garlic and stir-fry until just starting to colour. Add the prawns (shrimps) and stir-fry until just starting to turn pink. Add the oyster sauce, fish sauce and palm sugar. Cook until the sauces are blended. Add the cucumber and pepper and stir to combine. Pour the eggs into the wok and gently fold through the prawn (shrimp)mixture. Cook until just set, about 1 minute. Transfer to serving plate and garnish with the coriander (cilantro) leaves.

SERVES 2 AS A MAIN MEAL, OR 6-8 AS PART OF A SHARED MEAL

Royal Son-in-Law Eggs

So named because boiled eggs was the only dish a son-in-law could cook, and he had to think fast on his feet to feed his visiting mother-in-law. This is a royal version of an everyday dish that is enjoyed with a mound of rice.

Sauce:

2 tablespoons vegetable oil
250g (8oz) minced chicken
1 cup (250ml, 8fl oz) tamarind water
½ cup chopped light palm sugar
4 tablespoons fish sauce
2 green shallots (spring onion), thinly sliced

Eggs:

vegetable oil for deep frying
10 cloves garlic, thinly sliced
½ cup golden shallots (onion), thinly sliced
8 hard boiled eggs, shelled
2 medium red chillies, sliced
coriander (cilantro) sprigs to garnish

To make the sauce: heat oil to medium in a wok, add chicken mince and stir-fry until cooked. Add the tamarind water, palm sugar and fish sauce. Bring to the boil and then reduce to a simmer, cooking uncovered for a few minutes. Remove from heat and stir in the green shallots. Set aside.

To make the eggs: Heat some oil to low and deep fry the garlic until pale golden. Remove with a slotted spoon and drain on paper towel. Fry the shallots, stirring frequently, until golden, then drain on paper towel. Heat oil to medium and now fry the eggs until crisp and golden. This takes about 5 minutes. Remove with a slotted spoon and drain on paper towel. Cut eggs in half and arrange on serving platter. Reheat tamarind sauce and spoon over the eggs. Garnish with crispy garlic and shallots and tear the coriander (cilantro) sprigs over the eggs.

SERVES 8

Rice Soup with Egg

*This is like a Thai version of Jewish chicken soup,
as it's supposed to be a cure for the sick.
It's great also for breakfast.*

4 cloves garlic, thinly sliced

½ cup (125ml, 4fl oz)vegetable oil

1 litre chicken stock or water

1 cup cooked jasmine rice

250g (8oz) finely chopped chicken breast or lean pork

2 tablespoons oyster sauce

1 tablespoon fish sauce

1 teaspoon light palm sugar

4 eggs

freshly ground white pepper to season

1 cup bean sprouts

2 green shallots (spring onions, scallion), thinly sliced

handful of coriander (cilantro) sprigs to garnish

Heat oil in a wok to low and fry the garlic until pale golden. Remove with a slotted spoon and drain on paper towel. Strain oil and put aside to use in other dishes.

Bring the stock to boil in a saucepan, add the rice, chicken breast, oyster sauce, fish sauce and sugar. Simmer until the chicken is cooked, which takes only a few minutes. Taste and adjust seasoning if desired.

Break the raw eggs into 4 bowls. Divide the hot soup between the bowls, add a good pinch of pepper to each one then divide the bean sprouts, green shallots and coriander (cilantro) between the bowls.

SERVES 4

Sweet & Sour Chicken Omelette

A family favourite. Serve with a mound of steamed rice.

Filling:

2 tablespoons vegetable oil

5 mashed cloves of garlic

1 onion, cut in half and thinly sliced

250g (8oz) finely chopped chicken thigh

1 tablespoon oyster sauce

1 tablespoon fish sauce

3 large tomatoes, cut in half and finely sliced

1 red capsicum (sweet pepper/bell pepper), finely chopped

¼ cup palm sugar

Omelettes:

6 tablespoons vegetable oil

8 large eggs, lightly beaten

sprigs of coriander (cilantro) to garnish

To make the filling: heat oil in wok. Add garlic, stir-fry until golden. Add onion and stir-fry until softened.

Add the chicken meat, stir-fry until coloured. Add oyster sauce, fish sauce, tomatoes, capsicum (sweet pepper/bell pepper) and palm sugar. Simmer for 10-15 minutes. The sauce should be rather liquid. Set aside.

To make the omelette: heat oil in wok then add half of beaten eggs.

Let the eggs set for about 10 seconds then slowly rotate wok to distribute eggs in large circle. Cook until omelette is set, about 1-2 minutes.

Spoon half of filling into centre, fold omelette over the filling. Cook briefly, about 15-30 seconds. Using a spatula, slide the finished omelette onto an ovenproof platter and keep warm in a low oven. Repeat with remaining egg mix.

Garnish with coriander (cilantro). Serve with steamed jasmine rice

SERVES 4

Salads

[Yum]

Westerners tend to think of a salad as a side dish or a first course, but in Thailand salads are often part of a selection of dishes, eaten with rice as part of a shared meal.

Thai people prize 'yum' dishes because they are a perfect balance of the four flavours—hot, sweet, sour and salty. On local Thai restaurant menus, often the 'yum' section will be the longest.

Salads can be as rustic as a simple Som Tam from a street vendor, through to an elegant Royal Thai salad where the focus is on the interplay of many delicate flavours. Sometimes the 'yum' base is shredded green mango or green pawpaw (papaya), mixed with a handful of herbs such as mint, Thai basil, lemongrass and golden shallots, then tossed in a hot and sour dressing.

The most familiar 'yum' for Westerners is Yum Nua, a spicy Thai beef salad, but this barely scratches the surface of the salad range.

Other varieties include Yum Prik Chii Far, translated as 'sky pointing chilli salad', which as the name suggests, is the hottest. Yum Pla Duk Foo, made with dried shredded catfish, Yum Woon Sen, a noodle based salad, and Yum Thua Poo made with beans, are all examples of the many variations on the 'yum' theme. Yum Som O, is a famous salad made with pomelo, and is a popular inclusion on menus at upmarket Bangkok restaurants.

A cousin to 'yum' is Som Tum, a simple green papaya salad with a hot and sour dressing but with no added meat ingredients. The exception to Som Tum is Som Tum Buu, where a whole small raw crab—shell, claws and all—is pounded into the green papaya.

Out on the Bangkok streets, to find a 'yum' stall, look for a vendor with a mortar and a pestle—not the common wide, black granite mortar but a tall, narrow terracotta mortar with a long wooden pestle that is always used for making Som Tum. The dressing for the 'yum' is also made in these mortars.

Offerings

TEMPLE BIRDS

Outside many temples you will find vendors selling small red cages of birds.

Buying one of these cages and setting the birds free brings you good karma and good luck.

Apart from the food, nothing defines Thailand more than the sights, sounds and smells of the offerings at a local temple. To see and experience it all in one place, jump on the Bangkok Sky Train and take the On Nut line to Chit Lom station.

This brings you to the must-visit Erawan Shrine that is always packed with worshippers. Overflowing with scented flower offerings and blanketed in clouds of incense smoke, traditional Thai dancers and musicians add to the amazing atmosphere of this shrine.

The Brahma statue in the middle of the shrine is where Thais go to pray for luck in exams, lotto, business etc. Brahma has four faces that represent the four Dharma of Buddhism and offers help to people who come to him from all four directions.

The ritual is simple. Kneel down and say a prayer or make a wish, then place one quarter of your incense in the sand incense holder. Move to the next side of the statue and do the same, until you've completed all four sides.

If your wish comes true, return to the Erawan Shrine and pay the dancers to dance, as Brahma is known to be particularly fond of Thai dancing.

The items in Brahma's hands and their representations are:

- Book: Knowledge
- Beads: Controlling Karma
- Spear Stick: Will Power
- Flower Vase: Wish Fulfilment
- Conch Shell: Wealth and Prosperity
- Hand on Chest: Compassion
- Flying Wheel: Avert Disaster and Calamity, suppress Evil
- Cinta Mani: Power of Buddha Blessings
  (a fan used by
  monks for blessings)

In the old days, Thai people would eat with their hands ... which is hard to do elegantly. When European ambassadors arrived at the royal court with their cutlery, one of the early Thai kings adopted this new way of eating, making it easier to entertain foreign dignitaries and to show the world that Thailand was a cultured, modern kingdom.

With nothing really to cut in a Thai meal, the knife was superfluous, a fork and spoon were ideal for everything from soups to curries.

Chopsticks are usually used only when eating Chinese dishes like noodles.

Wild Mushroom Salad

Any type of mushroom can be used for this salad, depending on availability.

200g (7oz) assorted wild mushrooms.
¼ cup (60ml, 2fl oz) water
pinch of salt
pinch of sugar
4 tablespoons lime juice
3 tablespoons fish sauce
generous pinch roasted chilli powder
4 golden shallots, sliced
¼ cup mint leaves
¼ cup coriander (cilantro) leaves
2 spring onions (scallions), thinly sliced
1 tablespoon roasted rice powder

Clean and trim the mushrooms. Heat the water with the salt and sugar. Add the mushroom and simmer until cooked. Depending on the variety, the cooking time will need to be varied accordingly. Field mushrooms take 5 minutes, while oyster mushrooms need very little time. Remove from the heat and drain excess liquid.

Transfer to a bowl and add the lime juice, fish sauce, chilli powder, golden shallots, mint, coriander (cilantro) and spring onions. Toss to combine, transfer to serving plate and sprinkle with roasted rice powder.

SERVES 4

Som Tum Salad with Sticky Rice

A classic Thai salad is sold by street vendors all over Bangkok.

Dressing:

1 teaspoon peeled, chopped garlic

2 golden shallots, sliced

2 red chillies, chopped

3 teaspoons fish sauce

1½ tablespoons palm sugar

3 tablespoons lime juice

3 cups finely shredded green pawpaw (papaya)

200g (7oz) green beans, blanched and sliced

2 tablespoons dried shrimp

1 punnet of cherry tomatoes, halved

2 tablespoons roasted, crushed peanuts

2 cups sticky rice, soaked overnight in cold water to cover

Make the dressing: pound garlic, golden shallots and chilli to paste in mortar. Mix with fish sauce, sugar and lime juice.

To make salad: in large mixing bowl, combine the green pawpaw (papaya), beans, dried shrimp and tomatoes.

Toss with dressing, pile onto serving plate and sprinkle with peanuts for garnish.

To make sticky rice: drain water from rice, place rice in heatproof bowl. Place a trivet or vegetable steamer in base of a large deep saucepan.

Add enough water to steam, sit bowl on trivet, steamed covered for 25 -30 minutes.

SERVES 4

Banana Blossom Salad with Seared Chilli Squid & Chilli Lime Coconut

One of our most popular salads. This salad can be made with chicken or prawns (shrimps). If banana blossoms are unavailable, omit from recipe.

Squid marinade:

3 tablespoons fish sauce

1 tablespoon sweet soy sauce (kecap manis)

3 red chillies

2 garlic cloves

400g (14oz) baby squid, scored

Chilli, Lime and Coconut Dressing:

25g (¾oz) palm sugar

100 ml (3½fl oz) fish sauce

100 ml (3½fl oz) lime juice

50g (1½oz) Thai roasted chilli paste

50 ml (1¾oz) coconut cream

Salad:

6 white ends of shallots (spring onion, scallion), finely sliced

½ cup red onion, finely sliced

1 cup coconut zest

1 cup picked coriander (cilantro) leaves

1 cup crispy golden shallots

1 cup peanuts—unsalted, roasted and crushed

1 medium sliced banana blossom

3 large finely sliced red chilli

outer banana blossom leaves for garnish

To make the marinade: grind all ingredients in mortar and pestle to a paste.

Marinate scored baby squid in this mixture.

Sear marinated squid in a hot wok.

Drain and allow to cool slightly, before mixing into the salad.

To make the dressing: place palm sugar and fish sauce into a mortar and pestle and grind to dissolve sugar.

Add lime juice, chilli jam and slowly mix in the coconut cream.

Check seasoning and balance if necessary. Dressing should be salty but also sweet and tart.

To make the salad: combine all salad ingredients together, including the squid, and toss gently with the chilli, lime and coconut dressing.

Arrange on a plate using the outer banana blossom leaf as a cup.

SERVES 6

Cucumber Salad

A simple seasoned relish. This familiar side dish usually accompanies satays and is particularly refreshing with any deep fried foods.

Dressing:

½ cup white sugar

¼ cup (60ml, 2fl oz) rice or coconut vinegar

¼ cup (60ml, 2fl oz) water

1 teaspoon salt

Salad:

1 cucumber cut into quarters lengthways and then diced

1 small carrot, peeled and cut into quarters lengthways and thinly diced

1 golden shallot peeled and sliced

2 tablespoons ginger, peeled and shredded finely

1 large red chilli, finely chopped

2 tablespoons coriander (cilantro) leaves and stems, roughly chopped

Make the dressing: Combine sugar, vinegar, water and salt in a saucepan. Bring to the boil and cook uncovered for a few minutes. Remove from the heat and allow to cool.

Combine salad ingredients in a serving bowl and pour over cooled dressing.

SERVES 4-6 AS A SIDE DISH

Scallop, Eggplant & Peanut Salad

For a simpler version, just use roasted peanuts.

Dressing:

1 coriander (cilantro) root, cleaned
2 cloves garlic, peeled
2-6 medium red chillies, roughly chopped
1 tablespoon light palm sugar
1 tablespoon fish sauce
¼ cup (60ml, 2fl oz) lime juice

Caramelised peanuts:

2 tablespoons light palm sugar
1 tablespoon water
¼ cup roasted unsalted peanuts

16 scallops, roe removed if preferred
1 tablespoon vegetable oil
½ cup coriander (cilantro) leaves
½ cup mint leaves
½ punnet cherry tomatoes, halved
2 continental eggplant (aubergine), halved and char grilled until cooked, then cut into bite-sized pieces
1 teaspoon small dried shrimp, pounded in a mortar and pestle until fluffy
1 large red chilli, finely shredded
2 double Kaffir lime leaves, finely shredded

To make the dressing: combine coriander (cilantro) root, garlic and chillies in a mortar and pound to a paste.

In a bowl mix the palm sugar, fish sauce and lime juice together until the sugar dissolves. Stir in the paste.

To caramelise the peanuts: combine palm sugar and water in a small pan and cook gently until the sugar has dissolved, but don't stir. Keep cooking until the sugar starts to darken and caramelise. Add the peanuts and toss to coat with the caramel. Remove from heat and when cool crush coarsely.

To make the salad: heat vegetable oil in a heavy based fry pan until smoking and sear scallops for 1 minute on each side. This can also be done on a barbecue.

In a bowl combine the cooked scallops, coriander (cilantro), mint, cherry tomatoes, eggplant (aubergine), shrimp, red chilli, Kaffir lime leaves and dressing. Toss gently to combine then transfer to a serving plate. Sprinkle on the peanuts to garnish.

SERVES 4 AS AN ENTRÉE OR 8 AS PART OF A SHARED MEAL

Duck Salad with Citrus & Star Anise Dressing

A classic combination of duck and citrus.

Citrus Dressing:

1 cup light palm sugar

100 ml (3½fl oz) water

2 red chillies sliced finely

2 star anise

30 ml (1fl oz) soy sauce

250 ml (8½fl oz) freshly squeezed orange juice

zest of 4 oranges

coconut vinegar (if required)

Duck Salad:

1 duck breast (skin on)

½ cup coriander (cilantro) leaves

2 cups mixed salad leaves

½ cup bean sprouts

¼ cup finely sliced red onion

2 large red chillies, deseeded and thinly sliced

3 pinches garlic chives

4 each of orange and grapefruit segments (for garnish)

1 cup rice vermicelli noodles

To make the dressing: combine all ingredients in a pot. Bring to boil and reduce by two thirds. Remove star anise before using dressing and add some coconut vinegar if too sweet.

To make the salad: Roast duck breast in pre-heated oven 200°C (400°F, moderately hot, gas mark 5) for 10 minutes then set aside to rest.

Deep fry the noodles and set aside on kitchen paper to drain. They will double in size when frying.

Mix all salad ingredients in a bowl. Add in sliced duck breast.

Toss the salad with dressing. Serve with orange and grapefruit segments.

SERVES 2

Salad of Steamed Salmon with Yellow Bean & Ginger Dressing

Although salmon is not an Asian fish, its strong oily flavour holds up well against this robust dressing.

1 banana leaf, if available
500g (1lb) Atlantic salmon, skin off, pin bones out
1 cucumber, halved lengthways and sliced
1 punnet cherry tomatoes, halved
2 green shallot (spring onion, scallion), finely sliced
1 large red chilli, seeded and sliced
½ cup coriander (cilantro) leaves
½ cup mint leaves
1 tablespoon toasted sesame seeds
½ teaspoon roasted chilli powder

Line a steamer basket with banana leaf or grease proof paper. Make a few slits in the leaf to allow the steam through. Add salmon and place basket over wok half full of simmering water. Cover and steam gently until salmon is just cooked, about 7-10 minutes. Remove from heat and cool.

When cool, break salmon into large bite size pieces and place in large mixing bowl with the cucumber, tomatoes, green shallot (spring onion, scallion), chilli, coriander (cilantro) and mint leaves. Add ½ cup Yellow Bean and Ginger Dressing. Toss gently, transfer to serving plate. Garnish with sesame seeds and chilli powder.

SERVES 4

Yellow Bean & Ginger Dressing

This recipe makes a larger than needed quantity. It will keep in the fridge for a month and is also great for flavouring stir-fry dishes.

2 cloves garlic
2 medium red chillies, deseeded and chopped
½ cup ginger, finely shredded
½ cup (125ml, 4fl oz) light soy sauce
½ cup (125ml, 4fl oz) sweet soy sauce (kecap manis)
½ cup (125ml, 4fl oz) coconut vinegar
⅓ cup yellow bean sauce
⅓ cup palm sugar
½ teaspoon sesame oil

Make a paste with the garlic and chilli in a mortar and pestle, transfer to a saucepan with all the remaining ingredients. Bring to the boil and simmer a few minutes until the palm sugar is dissolved. Cool and then transfer to a clean jar.

Keep in the fridge.

MAKES 2 CUPS

Sweet & Sour Pickled Vegetable Salad

A cooling side dish to serve with spicy barbecued meats —or serve as a contrasting dish with rich curries.

Pickled vegetables:

1 carrot, julienne

½ cucumber, julienne

½ lime, thinly sliced

½ cup (125ml, 4fl oz) rice vinegar

½ cup (125ml, 4fl oz) water

1cup white sugar

1 teaspoons salt

Salad:

1 cup shredded Chinese cabbage

1 cups bean sprouts

2 spring onions, sliced

1 large red chilli, seeded and julienned

2 tablespoons Thai thin soy sauce to season

juice of 1 lime

2 tablespoons coarsely crushed roasted peanuts to garnish

To make the pickled vegetables: combine vegetables and lime in a large bowl. Bring vinegar, sugar, water and salt to the boil. Cool and then pour over the vegetables. Allow to pickle for at least 2 hours before using. Will keep in the fridge for about 1 week.

To make the salad: drain the pickled vegetables, keeping the liquid, and combine with the cabbage, bean sprouts, spring onion and chilli in a bowl. Dress with a ¼ cup (125ml, 4fl oz) of the pickling liquid, soy sauce and lime juice. Toss gently and sprinkle with peanuts.

Salad of Lobster with Lemon Grass & Coconut Dressing

If lobster is not available, prawns (shrimps), crab or scallops can also be used.

500g (1lb) cooked lobster meat
2 tablespoons fish sauce
3 tablespoons lime juice
4 tablespoons coconut cream
1-2 tablespoons light palm sugar
1 clove garlic, crushed
2 tablespoons ginger, peeled and finely shredded
2 Kaffir lime leaves, finely shredded
1 medium size chilli, deseeded and thinly sliced
2 stalks lemongrass, finely chopped
¼ cup coriander (cilantro) leaves and stems
2 tablespoons roasted and roughly chopped peanuts
lettuce cups for serving, allow 2 per person

Finely chop the lobster meat and set aside in refrigerator.

In a large mixing bowl combine the fish sauce, lime juice, coconut cream, palm sugar and garlic. Stir to dissolve the palm sugar. Add the lobster meat, ginger, Kaffir lime leaves, chilli, lemongrass and coriander (cilantro) leaves. Toss to coat with the dressing. Divide the salad between the lettuce cups and garnish with the peanuts. Transfer to serving platter. These are to be eaten by hand.

SERVES 4-6

Palm Sugar Cured Beef Fillet with Asian Noodle Salad

Cured beef:

750g (24oz) beef fillet, trimmed of fat and sinew

150g (5oz) light palm sugar, chopped

120g (4oz) sea salt flakes

4 coriander (cilantro) roots, cleaned and chopped finely

50 ml (1¾ fl oz) light soy sauce

Salad:

½ cup (125ml, 4 fl oz) white sugar

¼ cup (60ml, 2 fl oz) white vinegarr

1 carrot cut into thin strips

1 Lebanese cucumber cut into strips

½ daikon radish, cut into strips

125g (4oz) green beans, in 5cm lengths

1 red onion, thinly sliced

2 cups bean sprouts

2 large red chillies, deseeded and shredded

1 cup coriander (cilantro) leaves

125g (4oz) dried glass noodles, soaked in boiling water until soft. Then strain and refresh under cold water.

2 tablespoons toasted sesame seeds

Sesame Dressing:

100 ml (3½fl oz) peanut oil

½ tablespoon sesame oil

2 medium chillies, chopped

1 tablespoon ginger, chopped

2 cloves garlic, chopped

80 ml (2¾fl oz) light soy sauce

½ tablespoon sweet soy sauce

1 tablespoon mirin

juice of 1 lime

To cure the beef: combine all the ingredients and rub well over the beef. Place in shallow glass dish and cover with plastic wrap. Refrigerate for 24-36 hours. Turning every 8 hours. Remove from curing mix, wipe well with paper towel and then sear the beef in a very hot dry pan to brown well on all sides. Transfer to 200°C (400°F, moderately hot, gas mark 5) oven for 10 minutes. Remove from oven and rest. When cool refrigerate.

To make the salad: combine the sugar, vinegar, 1/4 cup of water and 1 teaspoon of salt in a saucepan, bring to the boil, remove from heat and cool. In a large bowl add the carrot, cucumber, radish, beans and onion. Pour over the cooled vinegar syrup. Allow to pickle for 2 hours. Then drain from syrup and combine with the bean sprouts, chilli, coriander (cilantro) leaves and noodles.

To make the dressing: heat the peanut oil and sesame oil and sauté the chilli, ginger and garlic until fragrant and lightly coloured. Remove from heat and when cool strain into a bowl. Whisk in the two soy sauces, mirin and lime juice.

To serve: slice the beef thinly and add to the salad. Add enough dressing to coat all the ingredients. Toss gently and transfer to serving plate, finish off with the sesame seeds to garnish.

SERVES 4-6

Puffy Catfish with Green Mango Salad

This is one of the best of the Thai salads. It also typifies how texture plays such an important element in Thai food. You would certainly get a surprise if you were expecting moist succulent fish, as the fish fillets are dried, shredded and then deep fried into a delicious crunchy, salty, crumble of fish. A little challenging at first but well worth the effort.

Puffy catfish:

400g (14oz) firm white fleshed fish fillets such as catfish, flathead or Nile perch

2 teaspoons salt

2 cups vegetable oil for deep frying

Dressing:

2-4 medium green chillies, chopped

2 tablespoons fish sauce

5 tablespoons lime juice

1 tablespoon light palm sugar

Salad:

1 green mango, peeled and julienned

2 golden shallots, peeled and thinly sliced

¼ cup mint leaves

¼ cup coriander (cilantro) leaves to garnish

¼ cup roasted peanuts or cashews, coarsely crushed to garnish

To prepare catfish: dry the fillets and rub with the salt.

Place on a rack in a roasting pan and bake the fish in an 180°C (350°F, moderate, gas mark 4) oven for about 30-40 minutes.

Allow to cool completely, then mix in a food processor until texture resembles fresh breadcrumbs. Don't overwork or the fish won't puff up.

Heat the oil in a wok to a moderate heat. Sprinkle on a handful of the fish and push together with a pair of tongs. When golden, remove to paper towel and repeat with remaining fish. Set aside, but don't make more than an hour or so ahead so that the fish remains crisp.

To make the dressing: crush the chillies in a mortar and then transfer to a bowl with the remaining ingredients. Stir to dissolve the sugar.

To assemble salad: in a large bowl combine the salad ingredients and the dressing. Gently toss to combine and then break up the fish into large pieces and toss briefly. Transfer to serving plate. Garnish with coriander and nuts.

SERVES 4-6 AS PART OF A SHARED MEAL

81

Noodles
[Swoy Teeo]

Noodles are the basic fast food of Asia. Noodle dishes can be purchased anywhere—on busy main thoroughfares, down back alleys and lane ways, even on rivers and canals.

Sold in sidewalk restaurants, by street vendors, by noodle boats and even by noodle bicycles, small bowls of noodles provide an instant, satisfying snack at any time of the day.

Noodles can be made from rice, eggs or soybeans and, just like pasta, come in different widths or shapes.

While each noodle recipe has its own ingredients, four small bowls are always set on the table so that each diner can adjust the noodles to their own flavour preferences.

The bowls always contain chillies in fish sauce ('nam pla prik'), chillies in rice vinegar ('prik nam som') sugar ('nam tan') and chilli powder ('prik pon'). Use them just as you would use salt and pepper to season a dish in a Western restaurant.

Green Leaves of Asia

For thousands of years, Asian food has been wrapped, cooked and served in a variety of aromatic leaves—banana, pandanus, ginger, water spinach, betel or herb leaves. These natural wrappers, easily grown in the village gardens, provided the perfect solution to environmentally friendly packaging.

Unfortunately, in many parts of Asia today, plastic litters the countryside and beaches, because the entrenched behaviour of throwing away natural wrapping makes no allowance for the fact that modern materials, such as plastic or aluminium foil, are not biodegradable.

Banana leaves are the aluminium foil of Asia! Pack, parcel, steam, bake—or shape a banana leaf to line a serving plate—their uses are endless. From wrapping sticky rice, desserts or fish, banana leaves are indispensable in Thai cooking. They can be purchased in packs at Asian supermarkets or green grocers.

Pandanus leaves provide a bright green essence that is used as a food colouring and for flavouring coconut milk in Thai desserts. Pandanus is also pressed into a cordial or syrup, mixed into refreshing drinks or just poured over ice. A favourite Thai snack is chicken pieces wrapped in pandanus strips then deep fried.

Betel leaves from the betel leaf plant, have no connection with the betel nut, which comes from a palm tree. Betel leaf is used like an envelope to wrap aromatic pastes and spices—including the famous paan served after meals in India.

'Cha plu', often incorrectly called betel, is part of the pepper family and the leaf used to wrap 'miang'. Easy to grow in a shady place, the leaves can also be added to green salads.

The aromatic leaves from the Kaffir lime tree have an intense flavour, and can be frozen or allowed to dry. Add a whole leaf to curries, or to the water when steaming rice, for a delicate lime infusion. Shred Kaffir lime leaves into hairlike slivers—just discard the woody stem, roll up the leaves into a cigarette shape and slice across very finely—and add to salads, stir fries and curries for a delightful citrus tang.

Herb leaves—mint, coriander (cilantro) and Thai, lemon and holy basils—are used prolifically in salads and stir-fry or as a garnish either whole, or chopped and scattered over the finished dish. The seeds of lemon basil can also be used in desserts. Easy to grow, cheap, and a good source of iron and calcium, the list of leafy Asian greens is endless ... water spinach ('pak boong'), 'choy sum', 'gai larn', 'pak choy', 'bok choy' to name just a few.

Don't make the mistake of adding these leafy greens to your Western style stir-fry. Because of their high water content, they will quickly turn a stir-fry into an Asian slush puppy! Cook all these leaves simply, in a hot wok with a few cloves of garlic and a splash of your favourite brown sauce—soy, yellow bean, or oyster—to enhance the flavour.

Black Bean Noodles with Marinated Tofu, Apple & Peanut Salad

A delicious vegetarian or vegan noodle dish.

Marinade:

¼ cup black beans, rinsed and drained

¼ cup (60ml, 2fl oz) Chinese rice wine

3 cloves garlic, peeled and crushed

¼ cup (60ml, 2fl oz) Hoisin sauce

1 tablespoon dark soy sauce

2 tablespoons light soy sauce

½ teaspoon dried chilli flakes

1 tablespoon finely chopped ginger

2 tablespoons sugar

¼ cup (60ml, 2fl oz) water

250g block firm tofu cut into 1cm (½ inch) pieces

Apple Salad:

1 apple, shredded

¼ cup mint leaves

¼ cup coriander (cilantro) leaves

juice of 1 lime

4 tablespoons coarsely crushed roasted peanuts.

To serve:

2 tablespoons vegetable oil

4 cups shredded Chinese cabbage

1 red capsicum (sweet pepper/bell pepper) cut into batons

½ red onion thinly sliced

2 cups bean sprouts, rinsed and drained

4 green shallot (spring onion, scallion) cut on the diagonal

100g (3½oz) snow peas, top, tailed and halved

500g (1lb) Hokkien noodles, blanched

To make the marinade: whisk all ingredients, except the tofu, together. Place tofu in a bowl and add half of the sauce. Toss to coat and put aside to marinate for 2 hours.

To make the Apple Salad: combine all ingredients in a bowl and toss to combine.

Heat the oil in a wok and then stir-fry the tofu and onion, add the remaining vegetables and the remaining sauce stir-fry briefly, mix in noodles and remove from heat.

Divide the noodles between four bowls and top with Apple Salad.

SERVES 4

Crispy Sweet Rice Noodles with Caramel Orange Duck

The classic 'Thai Mee Krob' has inspired this dish. At Spirit House, we cook a modern version using duck mince, but pork or chicken can also be used.

Caramel Duck:

1 tablespoon vegetable oil

250g (8oz) duck mince

125g (4oz) light palm sugar

1 tablespoon water

125g (4oz) fermented yellow beans, mashed

2½ tablespoons fish sauce

juice of 1 orange

Crispy Noodles:

2 cups vegetable oil

125g (4oz) rice vermicelli

2 eggs beaten

¼ cup garlic chives cut into 2.5cm (1 inch) lengths

1 red chilli, deseeded and cut into strips

zest of 1 orange blanched in boiling water.

2 golden shallot, sliced

1 head of Thai pickled garlic, skin removed and sliced

3 tofu puffs (deep fried tofu) cut into 1.25cm (½ inch) dice

2 cups bean sprouts, rinsed and drained

½ cup coriander (cilantro) leaves

To prepare the duck: heat the oil in a wok to a moderate heat and stir-fry duck until cooked. Combine palm sugar with the water in a saucepan and bring to the boil without stirring and cook until the sugar has caramelised slightly. Then add the yellow beans and fish sauce and cook until thickened. Remove from the heat and mix in the duck and the orange juice. Set aside.

To prepare the noodles: Heat vegetable oil in a wok to a medium heat. Pull the noodles apart and deep-fry in batches until puffed and crispy. Drain on absorbent paper. Pour most of oil from the wok and return wok to heat. Pour in egg and swirl to make a very thin omelette.

Roll omelette onto cutting board and when cool enough to handle cut into fine shreds. Set aside.

In a large bowl combine the garlic chives, chilli, orange zest, golden shallot, pickled garlic, tofu puffs, duck mince, bean sprouts and coriander (cilantro) leaves. Add the seasoned duck mince and toss gently to combine.

Break up crispy noodles and add to the mix along with the shredded egg. Combine and then transfer to serving plate.

SERVES 4

Asian Greens Stir-fry with Chinese Roast Pork, Basil & Egg Noodles

A complete noodle meal from our 'one bowl wonder' cooking class.

Chinese Roast Pork:

250g (1lb) pork neck

Marinade:

1 tablespoon fermented red bean curd

1 tablespoon light soy sauce

1 tablespoon Shaosing wine

½ tablespoon yellow bean sauce

1 tablespoon Hoisin sauce

1 tablespoon castor sugar

1 garlic clove, minced

Dressing:

1 tablespoon chilli jam

1 tablespoon light palm sugar

2 tablespoons lime juice

1 tablespoon fish sauce

1 teaspoon sesame oil

Stir-fry:

2 tablespoons peanut oil

3 golden shallots finely sliced

1 tablespoon ginger finely chopped

100g (3½oz) snow peas halved

1 bunch pak choy washed and roughly chopped

2 red chillies, seeded and sliced

1 tablespoon chilli paste

150g (5oz) fresh egg noodles blanched, refreshed and drained

½ cup of basil leaves to serve

To make Chinese roast pork: cut the pork neck into strips to resemble loins. Combine the marinade ingredients and pour over the pork. Marinate overnight if possible.

Preheat the oven to 240°C (500°F, very hot, gas mark 7). Fill a baking dish with water and cover with a cake rack. Place the pork strips on the rack (they should be suspended over the water) and roast for 45 minutes.

Cool and then slice thinly.

To make the dressing: whisk together the dressing ingredients and set aside.

To stir-fry: heat the peanut oil in a wok and on a moderate heat, fry the shallot and ginger until fragrant, about 1-2 minutes. Add the snow peas, pak choy and chillies and stir-fry over a high heat until wilted.

Add a tablespoon of water if necessary, then add the noodles, Roast Pork and Dressing ingredients.

Continue to fry until heated through. Fold through the basil leaves and serve immediately.

SERVES 6

Northern Style Noodle Soup with Chicken & Fried Bean Curd

A close relation to a Singaporean laksa, common in Chiang Mai markets.

Paste:

10 dried chillies, seeded and soaked in hot water till soft then chopped

2 large fresh red chillies, seeded and chopped

2 red onions finely chopped

60g (1¾oz) galangal, peeled and finely chopped

30g (1oz) ginger, peeled and finely chopped

3 stalks lemongrass, bruised and chopped

25g (¾oz) fresh turmeric, peeled and finely chopped

1½ teaspoons dried shrimp paste roasted

⅓ cup vegetable oil

2 teaspoons coriander (cilantro) seeds roasted and ground

½ cup dried shrimp soaked in hot water then drained and pounded finely

3 cups chicken stock or water

1 tablespoon fish sauce

1 tablespoon palm sugar

4 tablespoons Vietnamese mint finely chopped

2 chicken breast fillets thinly sliced

4 cups coconut milk

200g (7oz) dried rice vermicelli soaked in hot water till soft, drained

2 cups beans sprouts

100g deep fried bean curd, sliced

2 hard boiled eggs chopped

2 tablespoons crispy fried shallot

2 limes cut into wedges

Pound all the paste ingredients together in a mortar and pestle. Heat the oil in a wok and gently fry the paste over a low heat until fragrant and the oil starts to separate from the paste. Add the ground coriander (cilantro), fry for 1 minute then add the dried shrimp and fry another minute. Add the water, fish sauce, palm sugar and half the coriander (cilantro) leaf. Bring to the boil, simmer for 5 minutes then add the chicken. Simmer gently for another 5 minutes, add the coconut milk and almost bring to the boil then remove from the heat. Taste for fish sauce and palm sugar.

Arrange the noodles, bean sprouts and bean curd in bowls. Pour over the sauce and garnish with the rest of the coriander (cilantro), boiled eggs, lime wedges and crispy fried shallot.

SERVES 6

Hot & Sour Seafood Noodles

Commonly found in coastal markets, these spicy noodles use a mixed catch-of-the-day.

200g (6oz) firm fleshed white fish fillets, cut into 5cm (2 inch) pieces
8 green prawns (shrimps), peeled, leave tails on and heads if desired
8 scallops
500g (1lb) black mussels (clams)
200g squid, cleaned, scored and cut into 5cm (2 inch) pieces
2 tomatoes, peeled, seeded and diced
1 tray oyster mushrooms cut into bite size pieces
¼ cup fish sauce
1 tablespoon Thai roasted chilli paste
2 double Kaffir lime leaves, roughly torn
1 piece of lemongrass, cut into 5cm (2 inch) pieces
2-4 small hot chillies cut into thin rounds
½ cup (125ml, 4fl oz) lime juice
100g (3½oz) mung bean vermicelli (glass noodles) soaked in boiling water until softened
2 green shallot (spring onion, scallion), sliced
¼ cup coriander (cilantro) leaves

Prepare the stock. Reheat the stock in a large saucepan to boiling, reduce to a simmer and add the fish, cook for a minute, then add the prawns (shrimps), scallops and black mussels (clams), cover and cook for another minute.

Add the squid, tomatoes, oyster mushrooms, fish sauce, roasted chilli paste, Kaffir lime leaves, lemongrass and chillies.

Cook until the squid has curled and the mussels (clams) have opened. This should only take a minute or so.

Remove from heat and stir in the lime juice. Divide the drained noodles between 4 bowls and then divide the seafood and sauce evenly. Garnish with shallot and coriander leaves.

Stock:

1 litre (1¾ pints) chicken stock

2 stalks of lemongrass, bruised and cut into 10cm (4 inch) lengths

2 large dried chillies, roasted

4 slices peeled galangal

4 double Kaffir lime leaves

2 tablespoons Thai roasted chilli paste

1 tablespoons oyster sauce

2 coriander (cilantro) roots, cleaned and scraped

Bring the stock to boil add remaining ingredients and simmer for 5 minutes. Cool and then strain through a sieve or conical strainer into a bowl, discarding the solids.

SERVES 4

Vegetables

[Pak]

$\mathcal{P}$ractically every part of a vegetable is good enough to eat. Thai food uses roots like galangal, ginger or turmeric, edible leaves, seedpods like winged beans or sugar peas, blossoms of rosellas, banana flowers, or fruits such as egg plant or tomato.

There is one vegetable dish in Thailand that falls under the category of 'extreme cooking'.

If the idea of stir-frying petrol doesn't scare you, then you're ready to try 'pak boong fai daeng'.

This is a dish usually found at night markets … look for a wok with 6 feet (2 metres) of flame coming out of it and you're in the right place. The super heated cooking oil hits flash point imparting a slight burnt flavour to water spinach.

There are a few markets that specialise in flying 'pak boong fai daeng' … a vendor on one side of the street prepares the dish and then flings the wok full of 'pak boong' to a vendor on the other side of the street who catches it in his wok … most of the time!

Pickling

Pickling vegetables is very common in Thai cuisine, with pickles falling into two distinct categories, sour or salty. Pickling not only preserves the vegetables but intensifies the flavours. Pickles are usually served as a condiment or as a side dish, or are included in the actual cooking process. These are readily available from Asian supermarkets, but nothing beats the pleasure, or the taste, of making these pickles yourself.

Pickled Limes

12 limes cut into 2.5cm (1 inch) pieces
2 teaspoons plus 12 tablespoons vegetable oil
4½ teaspoons brown mustard seeds
1 teaspoon fenugreek seeds
30 curry leaves
300 ml (10fl oz) lime juice
2 teaspoons turmeric
2 teaspoons chilli powder
3 tablespoons salt

Put limes in saucepan, cover with water and bring to the boil for 1 minute. Discard water and repeat the process. Put the limes in fresh water and boil again, this time for 20-25 minutes. They should be tender and discolour. Drain and put aside.

Heat the 2 teaspoons of oil and add half of the mustard seeds and the fenugreek seeds. Stir and fry until the mustard seeds pop. Remove from heat and grind to a powder. Set aside.

Heat the 12 tablespoons of oil and add the remaining mustard seeds as soon as they pop add the curry leaves. Remove from heat and add the limes, lime juice, turmeric, chilli powder and salt. Mix well.

When cool place in sterilised jars or covered plastic containers. Cover and leave unrefrigerated for at least a week before using.

Refrigerate after 2 weeks. Keeps for up to one year.

Cucumber Pickle

1 peeled cucumber
2 large red chillies, thinly sliced
1 knob of ginger, thinly sliced
3 peeled golden shallot, thinly sliced
100 ml (3½fl oz) Chinese rice vinegar
100g (3½oz) caster sugar

Simmer vinegar and sugar until sugar is dissolved.

Cut cucumber in half, then using a vegetable peeler, peel cucumber into strips. (Remove seeds).

Mix the cucumber strips, chilli, ginger and golden shallot in a bowl and pour over vinegar and sugar mix.

Cool in refrigerator.

Pickled Vegetables

1 medium carrot
½ red capsicum (sweet pepper/bell pepper)
½ gold capsicum (sweet pepper/bell pepper)
12 baby corn
1 small red onion
1 cucumber
2 green chilli, sliced
50g (1½oz) finely sliced ginger
400 ml (14fl oz) rice wine vinegar
500g (1lb) palm sugar
20 ml (¾fl oz) fish sauce

Cut carrots, capsicums (sweet pepper/bell pepper), baby corn, red onion and cucumber into strips approximately the same size. Place into a bowl with the green chilli and ginger.

Bring rice wine vinegar, fish sauce and palm sugar to a simmer until the sugar has dissolved. Cool slightly and pour over vegetables. Allow vegetables to pickle for a few hours.

Pak Boong Fai Daeng

Wok of Fire

Super heated oil, garlic, yellow bean paste and chilli explode into sheets of flame when leafy water spinach is added to the wok. The end result is wilted greens with a smoky garlic flavour. While many restaurants have 'pak boong' on the menu, nothing beats eating it in a marketplace where the fireworks alone are worth the price of the dish. Be careful if you order this dish in the market—fiery chillies often hide in the tangle of leaves.

Some night markets in Thailand specialise in a flamboyant version of this dish where, after cooking, it's flung from the wok across the stall onto a plate being held by a waiter.

1 tablespoon vegetable oil
2 cloves garlic, coarsely crushed
1 large red chilli, roughly chopped
1 bunch water spinach, washed, or any leafy green Asian vegetable
1 tablespoon yellow bean sauce
½ teaspoon white sugar
1 tablespoon fish sauce

Heat oil to moderate and stir-fry the garlic and chilli briefly, add the water spinach, yellow bean sauce, sugar and fish sauce.

Keep stir-frying until spinach has wilted.

Transfer to serving plate. Or if feeling adventurous, fling across the kitchen to a plate on the dining room table!

SERVES 4 AS A SIDE DISH

Stir-Fried Bean Sprouts with Garlic Chives, Pork & Prawns

A typical Thai family stir-fry that is served as part of a selection of dishes.

2 tablespoons vegetable oil
3 cloves garlic, crushed to a paste
125g (4oz) finely diced pork fillet
125g (4oz) green prawns (shrimps), peeled, de-veined and finely chopped
2 tablespoons fish sauce
2 teaspoons sugar 200g (7oz) bean sprouts
200g (7oz) Chinese garlic chives, cut into 3cm (1½ inch) lengths
1 teaspoon freshly ground white pepper

Heat oil in wok to medium hot. Add the garlic and stir-fry briefly. Add the pork and prawns (shrimps), cook over high heat until cooked.

Add the fish sauce and sugar, then the bean sprouts and chives. Remove from heat, transfer to serving plate and sprinkle with white pepper.

SERVES 4

Stir-Fried Water Spinach with Nam Phrik Kapi

A variation of Pak Boong.

2 bunches of water spinach or similar Asian leafy greens
2 large red chillies, roughly chopped
2 cloves garlic, roughly chopped
1 golden shallot, chopped
1 x 3g (1/8 oz) slice of dried shrimp paste
3 tablespoons vegetable oil
1 teaspoon sugar
1 tablespoon soy sauce

Wash the water spinach, drain and set aside.

In mortar, pound the chillies, garlic, shallot and shrimp paste to a smooth paste.

Heat the oil in wok over medium heat.

Add the chilli paste and stir-fry for about 30 seconds. Add the water spinach and stir-fry until starting to wilt.

Add the sugar and soy sauce, stirring until well combined.

SERVES 4 AS A SIDE DISH

Stir-Fried Choy Sum & Vegetables with Yellow Bean Sauce

The keep-it-simple approach always works best with these vegetable stir-fry dishes.

2 tablespoons vegetable oil
2 cups seasonal vegetables, eg., snow peas, asparagus
1 bunch choy sum
3 cloves garlic, coarsely crushed
2 tablespoons yellow bean sauce
1 tablespoon fermented red bean curd (optional)
2 large red chillies, deseeded and cut into large strips
1 teaspoon palm sugar
1 tablespoon soy sauce
½ cup (125ml, 4fl oz) water or vegetable stock.

Heat oil to smoking, throw in the season vegetables and stir-fry for one minute, add the choy sum, garlic, yellow bean sauce, red bean curd if using, chillies and palm sugar. Stir-fry until the choy sum is wilted, then add the soy sauce and water or stock. Transfer to serving plate.

SERVES 4 AS A SIDE DISH

Roasted Banana Chilli & Eggplant Relish

Although traditionally this relish would be served as part of a banquet meal, it also makes a light, fresh appetiser.

4 long thin eggplant (aubergine)
2 banana chillies
1 tomato, peeled, deseeded and diced
2 red or golden shallots, finely chopped
1 large clove of garlic, minced
1-2 small green chillies, finely chopped
2 double Kaffir lime leaves, finely sliced
2 tablespoons lime juice
2 tablespoons fish sauce
2 teaspoons palm sugar
½ cup chopped coriander (cilantro) leaves

To serve:

1 cucumber, cut into slices
1 red capsicum (sweet pepper/bell pepper), sliced
50g (1½oz) snake beans or green beans, lightly blanched and cut into 10cm (4 inch) lengths

Grill eggplant (aubergine) on pre-heated barbecue until soft. When cool remove flesh and chop finely. Discard skin. Transfer flesh to a mixing bowl.

Grill banana chillies on preheated barbecue until skin is charred and blackened. When cool enough to handle remove skin and seeds and discard. Chop chilli finely and transfer to bowl with the eggplant (aubergine). Add the tomato, shallot, garlic, green chilli and Kaffir lime leaves.

In a separate bowl dissolve the sugar in the fish sauce and add the lime juice. Stir into eggplant (aubergine) along with the coriander (cilantro) leaves.

Transfer the dip to a serving bowl and serve with selection of sliced fresh vegetables.

SERVES 4 AS AN APPETISER

Shiitake Mushroom Wontons with Shallot Oil

Shallot Oil:

2 sliced shallot (spring onion, scallion) ends
(white ends only)

½ teaspoon sea salt

1 tablespoon ginger, finely sliced

100 ml (3½fl oz) vegetable oil

to garnish: 1 teaspoon soy sauce and 1
tablespoon toasted sesame seeds

400g (14oz) dried shiitake mushrooms
(soaked in warm water and drained)

10 ml (½fl oz) vegetable oil

25g (¾oz) pounded garlic

30g (1oz) carrot, finely chopped

50g (1½oz) bamboo shoots, finely chopped

50g (1½oz) bean spouts, finely chopped

50g (1½oz) snow peas, finely chopped

1 teaspoon ground white pepper

1 tablespoon chopped coriander
(cilantro) root

50g (1½oz) light palm sugar, crushed

60 ml (2fl oz) light soy sauce

50 wonton skins, defrosted

1 egg beaten

75g (2½oz) unsalted cashew nuts, roasted
and chopped

soy sauce and toasted sesame seeds to
garnish

To make Shallot Oil: place shallot (spring onion, scallion), ginger and sea salt in a mixing bowl. Heat oil in a wok until smoking.

Take off heat for 10 second and pour over shallot mix. Allow to cool.

Chop mushrooms in a food processor until finely minced.

Heat vegetable oil in a wok. Cook paste gently on low heat. Add chopped vegetables and cook until soft.

Mix in chopped mushrooms, palm sugar and soy sauce and cook over a moderate heat for 5 minutes. Place on tray to cool and fold through chopped cashew nuts.

To make wontons: place wonton skins on a bench a few at a time. Brush lightly with beaten egg and place a second skin overlapping diagonally. Place wonton skin in a small cup or mould and place 1½ tablespoons of mushroom mix into each of the moulds. Press mixture until firm in mould. Don't close the wontons at the top, but leave open.

Turn out from mould and place into bamboo steamer over wok of boiling water to cook.

Steam wontons over rapidly boiling water for 6-7 minutes.

Serve with Shallot Oil drizzled over each one with soy sauce and toasted sesame seeds.

SERVES 6-8

Stir-Fried Chinese Broccoli with Straw Mushrooms & Oyster Sauce

Straw mushrooms are difficult to buy fresh, but the tinned ones are suitable to use. They are also named 'paddy straw mushrooms' after their growing environment. They have a very high protein content.

2 tablespoons vegetable oil
4 cloves garlic, chopped
500g (1lb) Chinese broccoli, washed and trimmed
1 green chilli, chopped
½ cup drained canned straw mushrooms
2 tablespoons water
2 tablespoons oyster sauce
1 tablespoon fish sauce
1 teaspoon sugar
ground white pepper to taste

Heat oil in a wok to moderate temperature. Add the garlic and cook briefly until just starting to colour.

Turn the heat to high, add the broccoli, chillies and mushrooms and stir-fry until vegetables are starting to wilt.

Add the oyster sauce, water, fish sauce, sugar and pepper and stir-fry to combine.

Transfer to serving plate and serve at once as a vegetable side dish.

SERVES 4 AS A SIDE DISH

Curry
[Gaeng]

Charcoal Burners

Charcoal burners like this are the microwaves of Bangkok street food. Ideal for cooking and heating food, you see them everywhere, warming curries or firing woks of roasting chillies.

In the past, mangrove wood was the preferred timber for making charcoal but it has since been banned.

Charcoal is a great fuel for mobile street vendors because it is cheap, easy to carry and available at all the markets.

There's also the added flavour that charcoal smoke gives street food that you just don't find when cooking with gas.

300 years ago cooking pots and stoves like this ancient model would have been in every home in the ancient capital of Ayuddhaya. In fact the shape of the pot is still made to this day in the large tunnel kilns at Patumthani. These pots are used for serving and warming curries and soups.

You won't find the stove anymore, as it has been replaced with the bucket-like charcoal stove shown on the next page. But it is easy to see how a small fire in the hearth of this stove could be built and controlled. Air holes in the back of the stove help fuel the fire.

We discovered this cooking pot by accident on one of our Tag-Along tours ... an elderly Thai couple had collected a fantastic range of relics from the surrounding area of the old capital of Ayuddhaya and we stumbled on their shop while asking for directions.

They told us that Thai food back in the Ayuddhaya period was quite different to today, but dishes like 'tom yum' and 'tom kha gai' would have been popular and cooked in pots like this one.

On Phra Athit road near the Grand Palace is a restaurant called 'Hemlock' that specialises in cooking food from the Ayuddhaha period. Definitely worth visiting if you want to sample 'ye olde' Thai food.

COCONUT MILK

Coconut milk is processed by shredding coconut flesh from the coconut, mixing the flesh in a muslin bag with water and squeezing through a press.

This first pressing makes the coconut cream that has a high oil content, so it's perfect for using in curries.

The pressed bag of coconut flesh is then soaked in water again and pressed a few more times, producing a less creamy coconut milk used in drinks and desserts.

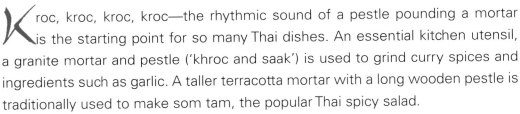

Kroc, kroc, kroc, kroc—the rhythmic sound of a pestle pounding a mortar is the starting point for so many Thai dishes. An essential kitchen utensil, a granite mortar and pestle ('khroc and saak') is used to grind curry spices and ingredients such as garlic. A taller terracotta mortar with a long wooden pestle is traditionally used to make som tam, the popular Thai spicy salad.

Working by sight, smell and touch, Thai cooks pound and grind a variety of pastes, which are used not only as a base for curries, but also for marinades, sauces, stir fries. Pastes are the building blocks of Thai cuisine.

Extremely functional, mortars are more effective for making pastes than a food processor, because the action of the two stones pounding together breaks down the cell structure, releasing all the juices, whereas the whirring blades of a food processor only chop the ingredients. Add a pinch of salt to the mortar to help release the juices.

When grinding spices, the action is more a milling technique, allowing the spices to roll around the mortar like the action of an old fashioned millstone, rather than a pounding.

Let the mortar and pestle do the work for you. Don't put your shoulder into it. You should be able to hold a glass of wine with one hand and pound effectively with the other, while not spilling a drop!

Steamed Red Curry with Prawns & Scallops

This is a popular curry, with the delicate cooking technique perfect for seafood. It's a great dish for dinner parties as the basket can be served at the table or the curry can be done in individual baskets.

Red Curry Paste:

(makes approximately 2 cups)
2 teaspoons coriander seeds, roasted
1 teaspoon cumin seeds, roasted
2 teaspoons white peppercorns
15 dried red chillies, soaked in hot water for 10 minutes
2 small red onions
12 cloves garlic
2 stalks lemongrass, finely sliced
1 tablespoon galangal, chopped
2 tablespoons coriander (cilantro) root, chopped
1 tablespoon lime zest
½ teaspoon mace, roasted
2 teaspoons salt
2 teaspoons shrimp paste, roasted

Red Curry Sauce:

2 tablespoons light palm sugar, shaved
2 tablespoons fish sauce
2 eggs, lightly beaten
3 cups coconut milk

To make the paste: in mortar and pestle, grind coriander, cumin and white peppercorns. Add remaining ingredients and pound until you have obtained a smooth paste. Store in a tightly sealed glass jar in refrigerator—keeps for two-three weeks.

To make the sauce: in a bowl mix the palm sugar and fish sauce until the sugar is dissolved. Add remaining ingredients and stir to combine.

To cook: bamboo steamer 30cm (12 inch) diameter, banana leaves, 1 cup Thai basil leaves, 16 large green prawns (shrimps), peeled, de-veined and heads removed, 24 scallops, 300g (11oz) good quality white fleshed fresh fish cut into thin medallions, curry sauce.

To garnish: 2 tablespoons coconut cream, 2 double shredded Kaffir lime leaves, 1 red chilli cut into fine strips, ¼ cup coriander (cilantro) leaves.

Trim banana leaves and soften over a flame and then line the steamer with the leaves making sure they overlap and cover the sides of the basket (otherwise the curry sauce leaks through). Now cover the banana leaves with basil and then cover the basil with the seafood. Pour over the curry sauce and place over a wok filled with boiling water. Steam until the sauce is starting to set and seafood is just cooked. This should take about 20 minutes.

Garnish with coconut cream, coriander (cilantro), Kaffir lime leaves and chilli.

Transfer the basket to a large flat plate and serve immediately.

SERVES 6

Kua Curry Paste:

6 large dried chillies, deseeded, soaked and finely chopped
1 teaspoon galangal, finely chopped
2 tablespoons lemongrass, finely chopped
1 teaspoon Kaffir lime zest
½ tablespoon coriander (cilantro) root, cleaned and chopped
2 tablespoons garlic, chopped roughly
2 tablespoons golden shallot, peeled and chopped
2 tablespoons dried mussels (clams)
generous pinch of salt

Prawn Dumplings:

¼ teaspoon white peppercorns
1 tablespoon coriander (cilantro) root, cleaned and chopped
1 clove garlic, peeled
2 teaspoons roughly chopped ginger
250g (8oz) fresh fish fillets, such as snapper, chopped finely
250g (8oz) green prawn (shrimp) meat, chopped finely
½ cup (125ml, 4fl oz) coconut cream
1 egg
1 tablespoon fish sauce

Curry:

2-3 tablespoons Kua paste
½ cup (125ml, 4fl oz)coconut cream
2 tablespoons vegetable oil
2 cups coconut milk
2 tablespoons palm sugar
2 tablespoons fish sauce
1 tablespoon tamarind water
2 cups fresh pineapple chunks
1 cup loosely packed Thai basil
4 double Kaffir lime leaves, roughly torn

To make the paste: combine all ingredients in a mortar and pestle and pound to a smooth paste.

To make the dumplings: first make a paste by grinding the white peppercorns in a mortar, then add the coriander (cilantro), garlic and ginger. Transfer fish mixture to the bowl of a food processor and process to a smooth paste. Add the coriander paste, coconut cream, egg and fish sauce. Pulse until just mixed. Add prawn (shrimp) meat and pulse briefly to combine. Transfer mix to a bowl and with wet hands form into 12 dumplings.

To make the curry: Combine the coconut cream and vegetable oil in a wok. Cook over gentle heat until the oil has separated from the cream.

Add the paste and cook gently until the paste is fragrant and mussels (clams) smell smokey. Add the palm sugar, fish sauce and tamarind water. Simmer to combine, then add the coconut milk. Bring to a gentle boil and poach the dumplings until just cooked, approximately 5-7 minutes.

Add the pineapple, basil and Kaffir lime leaves. Stir until basil has just wilted and transfer to serving bowl.

Kua Style Curry
with Sun Dried Mussels, Prawn Dumplings & Pineapple

Southern Style Green Curry of Swordfish with Bamboo Shoots & Ginger

This is a good example of southern style pastes that often incorporate fresh turmeric.

Green Curry Paste:

1 tablespoon coriander (cilantro) seed, roasted

1 teaspoon cumin, roasted

1 teaspoon mace

1 teaspoon white pepper, ground

½ cup chopped onion or golden shallot

6 cloves garlic

1 tablespoon chopped galangal

2 stalks lemongrass, bottom half only, finely chopped

5 large green chillies, seeded and chopped

6 small green chillies, chopped

4 coriander (cilantro) roots, cleaned, scraped and chopped

1 tablespoon krachai

1 tablespoon fresh turmeric, peeled and chopped

1 tablespoon lime zest

1 tablespoon shrimp paste, roasted

1 teaspoon salt

To make the paste: combine the spices in a mortar and pestle and grind finely. Add the remaining ingredients and pound to a paste.

Curry:

500 ml (16fl oz) coconut cream

3 tablespoons vegetable oil

4 tablespoons green curry paste

2 tablespoons finely shredded ginger

4 double Kaffir lime leaves

2 large green chillies, seeded and sliced

3 tablespoons fish sauce

3 tablespoons light palm sugar

2 tablespoons tamarind water

500g (1lb) swordfish, cut into 3-4cm (2 inch) pieces

½ cup bamboo shoots

1 punnet of baby corn

½ cup lemon basil

To make the curry: Remove 3 tablespoons of coconut cream from the top of the tin. Combine in a wok with the vegetable oil and cook over a low heat until the oil is released from the coconut cream. Add the paste and fry gently for 5 minutes.

Add the ginger, Kaffir lime leaves, green chillies, fish sauce and palm sugar. Stir for a minute to combine and then add the remaining coconut cream and tamarind water. Bring to the boil and then add the swordfish, bamboo shoots and baby corn

Simmer for 3 minutes, stir in basil. Transfer to serving bowl. Serve with steamed jasmine rice.

SERVES 4-6

Fragrant Red Curry of Tofu with Caramelised Sweet Potato, Cashews & Ginger

A delicious light curry that will appeal to vegetarians.

Red Curry Paste:

10 large dried chillies, deseeded and soaked in boiling water until soft, then chopped very finely

large pinch of salt

1 tablespoon chopped galangal

2 tablespoons chopped lemongrass

1 teaspoon lime zest

2 coriander (cilantro) roots, cleaned and scraped

3 tablespoons chopped onion

4 tablespoons chopped garlic

½ teaspoon white peppercorns, ground

1 teaspoon coriander (cilantro) seed, roasted and ground

½ teaspoon cumin seed, roasted and ground

1 teaspoon mace or ½ teaspoon nutmeg

To make the paste: combine all ingredients in a mortar and pestle and pound to a smooth paste.

To make the sweet potato: place the sweet potato on a large baking tray and toss with the oil, salt and pepper. Bake in a preheated 200°C (400°F, moderately hot, gas mark 5) oven until golden—about 45 minutes.

Caramelised Sweet Potato:

750g (1 ½lbs) sweet potato, peeled and cut into 5cm pieces
2 tablespoons vegetable oil
salt and pepper to season.

Curry:

2 tablespoons vegetable oil
2 cups coconut cream
1 tablespoons palm sugar
1 tablespoon light soy sauce
1 tablespoon sweet soy sauce
¼ cup finely julienne ginger
500g (1lb) firm tofu, cut into 2.5cm (1 inch) cubes
2 tablespoons tamarind water
½ cup Thai basil leaves
4 double Kaffir lime leaves, shredded, to garnish
1 long red chilli, shredded, to garnish
½ cup roasted and coarsely crushed cashews, to garnish

To make the curry: combine the oil and ¼ cup (60ml, 2fl oz) of coconut cream in a wok and simmer until the oil separates, about 5 minutes. Add 3 tablespoons of the curry paste and fry, stirring regularly over a gentle heat until fragrant. Add the palm sugar, both soy sauces, ginger and tofu cook a few minutes and then add the tamarind water and remaining coconut cream. Bring to the boil and then stir in the basil leaves. Remove from heat.

Place the caramelised sweet potato in a serving bowl. Pour over the curry sauce and then garnish with the Kaffir lime leaves, red chilli and cashews.

SERVES 4-6

Dry Red Curry of Cuttlefish with Wild Ginger, Snake Beans, Baby Corn & Basil

Phrik King Curry Paste:

(makes approximately 1 cup)

6 large dried red chillies

1 teaspoon whole white peppercorns

½ teaspoon salt

½ tablespoon minced fresh lime peel

1 large stalk of lemongrass, lower stalk trimmed and finely sliced

1½ teaspoon finely chopped, peeled galangal

¼ cup chopped garlic

½ cup chopped red onion

1 teaspoon shrimp paste, roasted

2 tablespoons vegetable oil

4 cloves garlic, coarsely crushed with a pinch of salt

1 tablespoons krachai (also known as wild ginger)

500g (1lb) cuttlefish, scored

bunch of snake beans, cut into 2.5cm (1 inch) lengths

1 punnet of baby corn cut in half

2 tablespoons palm sugar

2 tablespoons fish sauce

½ cup Thai basil or sweet basil leaves

To make the paste: soak chillies in warm water until softened. Set water aside. Grind peppercorns in mortar or spice mill, then add the salt. Finely chop remaining ingredients and transfer to mortar with the ground spices and shrimp paste. Pound to a paste using some of the chilli soaking water if necessary.

To make the curry: Heat vegetable oil in a wok to a low heat, fry the garlic until just starting to colour. Add 2-3 tablespoons curry paste and krachai and cook until fragrant, a few minutes.

Turn up the heat to high, add cuttlefish and stir-fry until just cooked—this only takes 2-3 minutes.

Add the snake beans, baby corn, palm sugar and fish sauce. Stir-fry a few minutes then add the basil and cook until the basil wilts.

Transfer to serving plates and serve with steamed jasmine rice.

SERVES 4

Coconut Braised Beef Shin in Jungle Curry Paste with Green Peppercorns & Kaffir Lime

One of the hottest Thai curries.

Jungle Curry Paste: (makes approximately 2½ cups)
1 teaspoon white peppercorns
3 tablespoons fresh large green chillies
1 tablespoon bird eye chillies
2 tablespoons coriander (cilantro) root and stem
1 tablespoon lime zest
1 tablespoon krachai
1 tablespoon shrimp paste, roasted
4 tablespoons golden shallot
4 tablespoons garlic
2 tablespoons galangal
4 tablespoons lemongrass, chopped
pinch of sea salt

Braised Beef:
½ teaspoon white peppercorns
3 coriander (cilantro) roots
3 cloves garlic
1kg (2lbs) of boneless beef shin
500 ml (16fl oz)
of coconut cream
2 tablespoons fish sauce
2 tablespoons palm sugar

Curry:
2 tablespoons vegetable oil
2-3 tablespoons jungle curry paste
2 tablespoons krachai
½ cup (125 ml, 4fl oz) water, or stock
2 tablespoons fish sauce
1 tablespoon palm sugar
4 double Kaffir lime leaves
1 punnet baby corn, sliced lengthwise
2 tablespoons coconut cream to garnish
2 tablespoons crispy shallot to garnish
thinly sliced red chilli strips to garnish
coriander (cilantro) sprigs to garnish

To make the paste: grind peppercorns in mortar and pestle. Add other ingredients and pound to a fine paste in mortar and pestle.

To braise the beef: grind white pepper in mortar, add coriander (cilantro) and garlic and pound to a paste. In heavy based saucepan, combine the coconut cream, paste, fish sauce and palm sugar, bring to boil. Add beef shin, cover and braise for 2 hours or until meat is tender. Remove and shred the meat.

To make the curry: heat oil in wok, cook 2-3 tablespoons jungle paste until fragrant. Add krachai and baby corn and stir-fry for one minute.
Stir in shredded beef, water, fish sauce, palm sugar and Kaffir lime leaves. Simmer until meat has warmed through. Transfer to serving bowl, spoon over coconut cream. Finish with shallot, chilli strips and coriander (cilantro) sprigs.

SERVES 6

Hot & Sour Orange Curry of Seafood & Pineapple

This rustic traditional curry is tangy, light and most refreshing.

Sour Orange Paste:

5 tablespoons garlic, chopped

10 dried, deseeded red chillis, soaked in warm water

1 cup golden shallot, peeled and chopped

2 teaspoons shrimp paste, roasted

6 dried shrimps

Sour Orange Sauce:

1 cup sour orange paste

30ml (1fl oz) vegetable oil

800ml (24fl oz) chicken stock

150ml (5fl oz) tamarind water

2 tablespoons palm sugar

2 tablespoons fish sauce

12 prawns (shrimps), peeled and de-veined

12 clams, open

200g (7oz) cuttlefish, cleaned, scored and halved

200g (7oz) black mussels (clams), cleaned

200g (7oz) white fish, diced

6 red chilli, halved and deseeded

1 cup snake beans

1 cup pineapple, sliced for garnish

12 Kaffir lime leaves, finely sliced

2 tablespoons lime juice

To make the paste: pound garlic in mortar and pestle. Add chilli, shallot, shrimp paste and dried shrimp and pound into a fine paste.

To make the sauce: in a heavy based pot, fry sour orange paste with vegetable oil until aromatic.

Add chicken stock, tamarind water and palm sugar.

Season with fish sauce and allow to simmer for 10 minutes.

Poach the seafood in the curry sauce and add chilli halves and snake beans. Simmer until cooked.

Finish with pineapple, Kaffir lime leaves and lime juice. Serve with steamed jasmine rice.

SERVES 4

Crispy Skin Spiced Chicken Breast in Fragrant Curry Sauce

This Spirit House favourite is a little complex but is well worth the effort!

6 large chicken breasts, skin on

Curry paste:

1 tablespoon roast and ground coriander (cilantro) seeds

1 tablespoon roasted shrimp paste

150g (5oz) deseeded large red chilli

50g (1½oz) peeled sliced garlic

250g (8oz) sliced red onions

60g (1¾oz) peeled sliced galangal (see ingredients p. 11)

25g (¾oz) peeled sliced ginger

90g (3oz) peeled sliced fresh turmeric

50g (1½oz) nuts (candlenuts, cashew nuts)

1 pinch ground nutmeg

80 ml (2¾fl oz) vegetable oil

1 tablespoon salt

water

To make the curry paste: Roast coriander (cilantro) seeds and shrimp paste and set aside to cool. Place all ingredients in a food processor and process until a smooth paste.

To make the curry sauce: On a low heat, fry the paste in the vegetable oil until fragrant. Add the other ingredients and allow it to come to a gentle simmer.

Remove from the heat and allow the sauce to stand and infuse.

To make the dry spice mix: Dry roast chilli, cumin seeds, coriander (cilantro) seeds, nigella seeds, mustard seeds and cardamom seeds over a gentle heat until fragrant. Cool and grind to a fine powder with white pepper.

Curry sauce:

25 ml (¾fl oz) vegetable oil

2 sticks lemongrass, crushed

4 Kaffir lime leaves, torn

2 teaspoons salt

1 teaspoon white peppercorns, ground

1 litre (1¾ pints) coconut milk

Dry spice mix for chicken:

5 dried red chillies

3 tablespoons cumin seeds

2 tablespoons coriander (cilantro) seeds

3 tablespoons nigella seeds

1½ tablespoons brown mustard seeds

1 tablespoon white peppercorns

10 cardamom pods

1 tablespoon ground cassia

1 tablespoon ground ginger

3 tablespoons sea salt

100g (3½oz) rice flour

Stir in ground cassia, ginger, salt and rice flour. (The spice mix can be stored for several weeks in airtight container and used for coating fish or lamb.)

To serve:

Dust the skin side of the chicken breast in the dry spice mix and pan fry until golden.

Turn the chicken over so the crisp skin side is on top.

Add the curry sauce to the pan and cover to half way on the breast leaving the top half out of the sauce.

Place the pan in a 200°C (400°F, moderately hot, gas mark 5) oven and allow the chicken to cook in the sauce.

SERVES 6

Penang Curry of Duck, Lotus Root & Red Grapes

The surprising touch of grapes add a beautiful sweetness to counterbalance the heat of this curry. The lotus root makes an interesting alternative to bamboo shoots.

2 cups of coconut cream
3 tablespoons red curry paste
2 tablespoons fish sauce
2 tablespoons palm sugar
1 Chinese roast duck, boned and sliced (from any Chinese BBQ shop)
½ cup roasted and crushed peanuts
2 large red chillies, halved and deseeded
6 Kaffir lime leaves
200g (½ lb) sliced green beans
1 cup loosely packed basil leaves
½ jar lotus root (available at Asian supermarkets in jars or frozen packs)
½ cup seedless red grapes, stems removed

Skim off half a cup of coconut cream and boil in wok until starting to separate.

Add the red curry paste and fry for five minutes, stirring constantly.

Add fish sauce and palm sugar and cook for 3-4 minutes.

Add remaining coconut cream and bring to boil.

Add duck and remaining ingredients and simmer for 2-3 minutes.

Served with steamed jasmine rice.

SERVES 4

Seafood
[Aharn talay]

Thai food is a celebration of the life-giving power of water. The lives of most Thai people are closely interwoven with water. Bangkok was formerly known as the Venice of the East because of its vast network of canals, most of which have now been turned into freeways and roads.

Villages spread along tree lined canals, 'klongs', ponds and rivers or nestle amongst the palm trees on the ocean shore. Water gives life—irrigation for the rice paddies, water insects and reeds for ducks to forage on, vegetables such as water chestnut, lotus and water spinach spread out across the ponds, while a wide variety of fish, shell fish and squid provide a reliable and cheap source of protein for the daily diet. Nam Pla (literally 'fish water'), the ubiquitous fish sauce without which a Thai meal would not be complete, is fermented in barrels from tiny anchovies netted from the sea.

Seafood Stir-fried in Tom Yum Paste

The coloured prawn and mussel shells make this a most attractive spicy stir-fry. Serve in a wide shallow bowl at the table together with coconut rice.

Tom Yum Paste:

3 red chilli, sliced with seeds

3 green chilli, sliced with seeds

3 garlic cloves

75 ml (2½fl oz) vegetable oil

250g (8oz) chilli paste with soy bean oil (buy in jars from Asian supermarkets)

100 ml (3½fl oz) fish sauce

Stir-fry mix:

12 green prawns (shrimps), peeled and deveined

24 mussels (clams)

250g (½lb) cuttlefish, cleaned, scored and halved

¾ cup (185ml, 6fl oz) chicken stock

6 red chilli, halved and deseeded

1 cup snake beans

12 baby corn, halved

¼ cup golden shallot, finely sliced

12 Kaffir limes leaves

3 tablespoons fish sauce

3 tablespoons palm sugar

2 tablespoons lime juice

1 cup basil

To make the paste: pound chilli and garlic in a mortar and pestle. Transfer into a heavy based pot with vegetable oil and cook on a very low heat for 5 minutes. Add chilli paste and cook for a further 10 minutes. Season with fish sauce and remove from heat.

To make the stir-fry: Stir-fry seafood in a little vegetable oil in a hot wok. If the mussels do not open, leave them in the wok but do not eat them. Eat only the opened ones.

Add 8 tablespoons of Tom Yum paste and stir-fry for 2 minutes. Add chicken stock, chilli halves, snake beans, baby corn, golden shallot and Kaffir lime leaves. Season with fish sauce and palm sugar and stir-fry until seafood and vegetables are cooked. Finish with lime juice and Thai basil. Serve with steamed jasmine rice or coconut rice.

SERVES 4-6

Poached Red Snapper with Hot & Sour Herb Salad

A fragrant, light main course for easy entertaining.

Poaching liquid:

200 ml (7fl oz) fish sauce

200 ml (7fl oz) lime juice

100g (3½oz) palm sugar

6 x 200g (7oz) portions of red snapper or other white fish

Hot and Sour Herb Salad:

4 red chillies

4 green chillies

2 birds eye chillies

6 garlic cloves

4 coriander (cilantro) roots, cleaned

1 cup coriander (cilantro) leaves

½ cup mint leaves

1 cup bean sprouts

To make the poaching liquid: grind palm sugar in a mortar and pestle with fish sauce and lime juice until the sugar dissolves.

Pour all, except for 2 tablespoons, of poaching liquid mixture over the fish fillets and place in baking dish, cover with foil and steam in a moderate oven (180°C, 350°F, gas mark 4) for approximately 6 minutes.

To make the hot and sour salad: Pound chillies, garlic and coriander (cilantro) root in mortar and pestle with remaining 2 tablespoons of poaching liquid. Mix with coriander (cilantro), mint leaves and bean sprouts and garnish cooked fish with this salad.

SERVES 6

137

Char Grilled Garlic & Pepper Prawns with Green Chilli Sauce & Mango, Coconut, Ginger Relish

If mangos are out of season, red papaya is an alternative.

Green Chilli Dipping Sauce:

1 tablespoon coriander (cilantro) root and stem

2 cloves garlic

5 small green chillies

2 tablespoons lime juice

1 teaspoon palm sugar

1 tablespoon fish sauce

Mango, Coconut and Ginger Relish:

2 mangos, peeled and diced

2 green shallot (spring onion, scallion), finely sliced

1 large red chilli, finely chopped

2 tablespoons ginger, peeled and sliced

¼ cup coarsely grated fresh coconut

½ cup mint leaves, finely chopped

1 teaspoon grated light palm sugar

2 tablespoons lime juice

1 tablespoon fish sauce

1 teaspoon whole white peppercorns

½ cup coriander (cilantro) root and stem

6 cloves garlic

1 teaspoon of palm sugar

1 tablespoon of fish sauce

1kg (2lb) green prawns (shrimps), leave in shell, split down back and deveined

To make the dipping sauce: in mortar, crush coriander (cilantro), garlic and chillies.

Add lime juice, sugar and fish sauce. Mix well.

To make the relish: combine mango, shallot (spring onion, scallion), red chilli, ginger, coconut and mint in a mixing bowl.

In a separate bowl dissolve the palm sugar with the lime juice and fish sauce. Add to the mango and stir to combine. Let stand for an hour or so for the flavours to combine.

Pound white peppercorns, coriander (cilantro) and garlic to a paste. Dissolve palm sugar and fish sauce, stir into paste. Add prawns (shrimps), toss well, marinate for 2 hours.

Cook prawns (shrimps) on medium barbecue heat, about 1 minute on either side. Serve on platter with Green Chilli Dipping sauce and bowl of Mango, Coconut and Ginger Relish.

SERVES 4-6

Barbecued Squid Stuffed with Pork

Pork and seafood are a very popular combination in Thai cuisine. Serve as an entrée or part of a shared banquet meal.

Hot and Sour Dipping Sauce:

1 birds eye chilli, including seeds

1 clove garlic

1 tablespoon palm sugar

2 tablespoons lime juice

2 tablespoons fish sauce

1 teaspoon chopped coriander (cilantro) leaves

5 coriander (cilantro) roots washed, scraped and chopped

2 cloves garlic chopped

½ teaspoon white peppercorns ground

1 teaspoon sea salt

1 tablespoon fish sauce

500g (1lb) pork mince

3 lime leaves, finely shredded

2 tablespoons roasted and crushed peanuts

8 medium sized squid tubes

Salad:

6 cos lettuce leaves shredded

1 carrot, finely sliced

handful bean sprouts

½ cup coriander (cilantro) leaves

½ cup Thai basil leaves

Make the dipping sauce: pound the chilli and garlic together in a mortar. Blend in the palm sugar, lime juice, fish sauce and coriander (cilantro) leaves.

In a mortar and pestle, make a paste with the coriander (cilantro) roots, garlic, white pepper and salt.

Stuff the squid: Combine paste, fish sauce, pork mince, lime leaves and peanuts in a bowl.

Stuff the squid with the pork mixture—about two thirds full to allow for expansion. Steam for 10 minutes over boiling water. Cook the squid on a well oiled barbecue flat plate to brown all over—about 6 minutes.

Toss together the salad ingredients and place on a plate.

Cut the hot squid tubes into diagonal slices and arrange on top.

Drizzle the dipping sauce over the top of squid and serve extra sauce in bowl on the side.

SERVES 6

Miang of Scallops

This unusual appetiser, traditionally made with Cha Plu leaves, a wild betel leaf, illustrates the wonderful contrast of flavours found in Thai cuisine.

2 tablespoons roasted, crushed peanuts
½ cup sliced golden shallot
½ stalk lemongrass, tender part only
finely chopped
1-2 fresh red chillies, deseeded and finely chopped
1 tablespoon finely chopped ginger
1 lime, peeled, remove all pith, cut into 5cm
(2 inch) pieces
200g (7oz) of cooked scallops, chopped
1 bunch of cha plu leaves (if unavailable use butter
lettuce or spinach (silver beet) leaves)

Sauce:
1 tablespoon palm sugar
1 tablespoon lime juice
1 tablespoon tamarind water
2 tablespoons dried shrimp
1 clove garlic, finely chopped
(makes about 20)

Combine all the remaining ingredients in bowl, except the cha plu.

To make the sauce, combine all the ingredients in a bowl.

Arrange cha plu leaves on serving platter, and spoon filling onto each leaf. Spoon sauce over each one.

SERVES 4-6

Barbecue Tuna with Lemongrass Dressing

Just beautiful! If tuna is unavailable use a meaty fish such as mahi-mahi or swordfish.

Lemongrass Dressing:

6 golden shallots, cut in half, peeled and finely sliced

4 cloves of garlic, crushed in a mortar and pestle with a pinch of salt

2-6 small red chillies, finely chopped

4 double Kaffir lime leaves, finely shredded

1 teaspoon shrimp paste, roasted

4 stalks of lemongrass, bottom half only, outer layer removed then finely chopped

1 teaspoon salt

2 tablespoons lime juice

⅓ cup vegetable oil

black pepper to season

500g (1lb) tuna steaks

½ cup red curry paste

1 teaspoon salt

½ teaspoon freshly ground black pepper

1 tablespoon lime juice

2 tablespoons vegetable oil

crispy fried shallot to garnish

To make the dressing: combine all ingredients a mixing bowl and stir well to combine.

Season tuna with the red curry paste, salt, pepper and lime juice.

Heat the barbecue, brush with the oil and cook tuna for 3 minutes on each side.

Set aside to cool, then break into small chunks into a mixing bowl, add 1 cup Lemongrass Dressing and mix well.

Adjust seasoning with salt and pepper to taste. Transfer to serving plate and sprinkle with fried shallot.

SERVES 4-6

Fried Mussel Pancake

MAKES 2 LARGE PANCAKES

1½kg (3lb) black mussels (clams)
½ cup (125ml, 4fl oz)water

Pancake Batter:

3 tablespoons rice flour
3 tablespoons plain flour
¼ teaspoon salt
1 egg
1 cup (250ml, 8fl oz)water

Sauce:

2 teaspoons soy sauce
1 tablespoon fish sauce
1 teaspoon white sugar

6 tablespoons vegetable oil
1 garlic clove finely chopped
1 egg, beaten
pinch white pepper
handful bean sprouts
1 green shallot (spring onion,
scallion) finely sliced
½ cup coriander (cilantro) leaves
for garnish

Put the mussels and water in a pot, cover and cook over a high heat until the mussels (clams) have opened.

Drain and when cool, remove the mussels (clams) from their shells.

To make the pancake batter: mix together the flours and salt in a bowl. Stir in the egg and then the water to form a smooth batter, the consistency of milk.

Add mussels (clams) to the batter.

To make the sauce: mix sauces and sugar together in a bowl.

Heat half the oil in a flat pan and fry half the garlic until fragrant. Pour in half the mussels (clams) and half the batter and cook one side.

Tip the mixture around to distribute the batter evenly. When the mixture has set and is starting to crisp on the bottom, shake the pan to loosen the pancake, then using a spatula or wok shovel, tear the pancake into 5 or 6 pieces. Turn the pieces over and continue to fry, adding a little more oil if needed. Fry and turn the pieces for a few minutes until they are brown and crispy all over.

Pour over half the beaten egg, turn off the heat and sprinkle over half the soy sauce mixture, white pepper, half bean sprouts and half green shallot (spring onion, scallion).

Turn to combine, then pile on a plate. Garnish with the coriander (cilantro). Repeat the process with the remaining mussels (clams), batter and ingredients.

Serve with bowl of sweet chilli sauce on the side (see index).

SERVES 4

Seared Scallops, Pickled Vegetables with Chilli, Soy Bean & Tamarind Sauce

Pickled vegetables:

1 medium carrot

½ red capsicum (sweet pepper/bell pepper)

½ gold capsicum (sweet pepper/bell pepper)

12 baby corn

1 small red onion

1 cucumber

2 green chilli, sliced

25g (¾oz) finely sliced ginger

200 ml (7fl oz) rice wine vinegar

250g (8oz) palm sugar

1 tablespoon fish sauce

Tamarind Sauce:

250g (8oz) chilli paste and soy bean oil (available in jar from Asian supermarkets)

60 ml (2fl oz) tamarind water

50 ml (1¾fl oz) tomato ketchup

150 ml (5fl oz) coconut cream

1 tablespoon sugar

12 scallops in half shell (roe off)

10 ml (½fl oz) vegetable oil

finely sliced chilli and coriander (cilantro) to garnish

rock salt and Szechwan peppercorns to garnish

To make the pickled vegetables: cut carrot, capsicum (sweet pepper/bell pepper) , baby corn and red onion into 4cm (½ inch) strips approximately the same size. Place into a bowl with the green chilli and ginger.

Bring rice wine vinegar, fish sauce and palm sugar to a simmer until the sugar has dissolved. Cool slightly and pour over vegetables. Allow vegetables to pickle for a few hours.

To make the sauce: in a heavy based pot, sauté chilli paste until fragrant. Add tamarind water, sugar and tomato ketchup and simmer for 5 minutes. Add coconut cream and simmer for a further 5 minutes.

Remove scallops from half shells. Pan fry scallops in vegetable oil until caramelized but still slightly undercooked—about 30 seconds. Place a few spoons of the prepared chilli and tamarind sauce in the pan and finish cooking until scallops are firm.

To serve: Clean scallop shells and arrange on a bed of rock salt with some Szechwan peppercorns mixed through. Place a small amount of the vegetable pickle in each shell and then one scallop. Finish with reduced Tamarind Sauce and garnish with coriander and chilli.

SERVES 4

Fried Garlic & Coriander Reef Fillets with Lime Chilli Sauce

Lime Chilli Sauce:

2 tablespoons lime juice

1 tablespoon fish sauce

1 tablespoon sliced birds eye chillies

1 tablespoon soya sauce

1 tablespoon fish sauce

1 teaspoon palm sugar

500g (1lb) of reef fillets (eg., snapper, red emporer), cut into approximately 50g (1½oz) strips

2 tablespoons rice flour

Paste:

¼ cup coriander (cilantro) root and stem

½ teaspoon white peppercorns

½ cup of peeled garlic, roughly chopped

1 teaspoon ginger, roughly chopped

4 cups of vegetable oil

½ cup coriander (cilantro) leaves to garnish

To make the sauce: mix all ingredients together in small dipping bowl.

Combine soya, fish sauce and sugar. Marinate the fish pieces in the mixture for about 30 minutes.

Remove fish from marinade, toss fish pieces in rice flour.

To make the paste: Make a paste in mortar and pestle with the coriander (cilantro) roots, peppercorns, garlic and ginger.

Heat 4 cups of vegetable oil in wok until hot, add the fish pieces and paste, deep fry until golden brown and crisp. Remove from wok with skimmer, drain on paper towel.

Transfer to serving plate, garnish with coriander (cilantro) leaves. Serve with Lime Chilli Sauce.

SERVES 4

Salt & Pepper Tempura Prawns with Green Mango Relish

Salt and Pepper Mix:

1 teaspoon Szechwan pepper, roasted

2 teaspoons coriander (cilantro) seed, roasted

1 teaspoon white peppercorns

½ teaspoon five spice powder

2 tablespoons sea salt

Mango Relish:

1 green mango, sliced

1 medium red chilli, chopped

¼ cup coriander (cilantro) leaves and stems, roughly chopped

¼ cup mint leaves, shredded

2 tablespoons lime juice

2 tablespoons light palm sugar

1 tablespoon fish sauce

Tempura Prawns:

12 large green king prawns (shrimps), peeled, de-veined and tails left on

½ cup rice or cornflour

½ cup self-raising flour

1 cup (250ml, 8fl oz) soda water

4 cups vegetable oil for deep frying

½ cup plain flour

1-2 teaspoons salt and pepper mix

To make the salt and pepper mix: grind the whole spices and combine with the five spice powder and sea salt. This can be made in advance and stored in a airtight jar.

To make the relish: combine mango, chilli, coriander (cilantro) and mint in a bowl. In a separate bowl mix the lime juice, sugar and fish sauce, stirring to dissolve the sugar. Pour into mango mix and toss to combine.

To make the tempura: Combine rice and self-raising flour in a bowl add the soda water and stir to combine.

The batter should have the consistency of pouring cream.

Heat the oil in a wok to a medium heat and toss the prawns (shrimps) in the plain flour and then into the tempura batter.

Cook for 3-4 minutes until the batter is pale golden and crisp. Remove from oil with a slotted spoon and drain on absorbent paper.

Transfer to serving plate and sprinkle with the salt and pepper mix.

Serve the Mango Relish on the side

SERVES 4 AS AN ENTRÉE OR 6 AS PART OF SHARED MEAL

Chicken

[Gai]

&

Duck

[Bped]

During the day on Bangkok streets, you will find a variety of satays, ranging from Isaan sausage satay to chicken feet satay.

But vendors of satay with peanut sauce tend to be nocturnal animals, emerging at dusk to feed hungry office workers with tasty marinated chicken or pork satay in a delicious peanut sauce. Look for their long charcoal burners bristling with bamboo skewers of pork or chicken and you've found snack heaven.

Satay is usually sold by the stick or 'mai', and served with tasty Thai peanut sauce and cooling cucumber relish. Ask the vendor to 'sai toong' which means to put them in a bag.

Satay also forms part of Thai food known as 'kap klaem' which translates as drinking food. At the end of a hot tiring day, find a satay stall, buy a bag of satay sticks and head to your hotel. Grab a cold Singha beer from the mini bar, put your feet up and enjoy.

A perfect way to recharge your batteries before you head out to one of Bangkok's fantastic restaurants or night markets.

master stock

Master stock is a delicious concoction in which the ingredients are first cooked and allowed to cool in the liquid allowing the flavour to permeate throughout. Once started, it can be used over and over again for poaching fish, fowl and cuts of meat. The stock can be reduced down to make a rich, luscious sauce.

In China, some master stocks are handed down as wedding presents and can be generations old because the stock is boiled and continually added to for the next use. See Braised Duck in Chinese Star Anise Sauce for one stock recipe.

Peanut Satay Sauce

Satays are found throughout South East Asia with each country adding their own culinary magic. This sauce takes its inspiration from Malaysia. The Thai version adds even more richness with coconut milk and the classic Thai seasoning of fish sauce.

MAKES 3½ CUPS

Paste:

6 dried chillies, deseeded

1 tablespoon galangal peeled and chopped

2 stalks lemongrass finely chopped.

(use only the bottom half and discard 2-3 outer layers)

¼ cup finely chopped golden shallot

4 cloves garlic, peeled and chopped

1 teaspoon shrimp paste, roasted

2 teaspoons ground coriander (cilantro)

1 teaspoon ground cumin

½ teaspoon turmeric

Sauce:

¼ cup (60ml, 2fl oz) vegetable oil

2 tablespoons thick tamarind water

2 tablespoons dark palm sugar

1 teaspoon salt or to taste

1½ cups roasted and ground peanuts

1½ cup (375ml, 12fl oz) water

To make the paste: soak dried chillies in boiling water until softened. Finely chop and then combine with remaining paste ingredients in a mortar and pound to a smooth paste.

To make the satay sauce: heat oil in a wok and stir-fry the paste until fragrant. Add remaining sauce ingredients and simmer until thick.

Pineapple Satay Sauce

An alternative sauce to serve with pork satays.

½ pineapple, peeled, cored and chopped finely
1 large red chilli, finely chopped
1 tablespoon white sugar
2 teaspoons lime juice
¼ teaspoon salt

Combine all ingredients in a bowl and rest in refrigerator for ½ hour before using.

SERVES 4-6

Chicken Satays

Paste:

1 stalk lemongrass, peeled and chopped
5 golden shallots, peeled and chopped
2 teaspoons coriander (cilantro) seeds, roasted and ground
1 teaspoon cumin seeds, roasted and ground
1 teaspoon turmeric powder
¼ teaspoon cinnamon or ground cassia
1 teaspoon salt
2 teaspoons palm sugar
2 tablespoons roasted peanuts
1 tablespoon vegetable oil

500g (1lb) chicken thigh (or pork neck can be used if preferred), sliced into strips
20 bamboo satay sticks soaked overnight in water

To make the paste: prepare the paste by pounding all ingredients in a mortar in pestle to a smooth paste.

Mix the meat and paste in a bowl and marinate for 2 hours, then thread onto bamboo sticks.

Barbeque sticks over medium heat for about 15-20 minutes, turning the satays often.

Transfer to a serving plate and serve with peanut sauce and cucumber relish.

SERVES 4-6

Stir-Fried Chicken with Holy Basil

A rustic and fiery stir-fry eaten in markets throughout Thailand. Usually served with rice and often topped off with a fried egg. If holy basil is unavailable, use Thai basil or mint.

8 cloves garlic, peeled and chopped

2 medium chillies, red or green, sliced

2-6 small birds eye chillies, red or green, sliced

2 tablespoons vegetable oil

2 sliced golden shallots

400g (12oz) chicken mince or finely chopped thigh meat

1 tablespoons fish sauce

1 tablespoon soy sauce

1 tablespoons palm sugar

1 tablespoon sweet soy sauce

1 cup of holy basil, or Thai basil or mint leaves

lime wedges

Make a paste with the garlic and chillies. Heat oil in a wok to medium and cook the paste for a minute. Add the golden shallot and cook until starting to soften. Add the mince and stir-fry for a few minutes. Next add the fish sauce, soy sauce, palm sugar and sweet soy. Keep cooking until the sauces have combined and the meat is cooked. Stir through the basil and remove from heat. Transfer to plates and serve with lime wedges.

SERVES 4

Chicken & Bean Curd Rolls with Cucumber Pickle

Bean curd skins are available from Asian supermarkets. They can be very salty, so rinse thoroughly before using. The skins are made from the curd that forms on the surface of soya milk when it is heated.

1 packet bean curd skins

Chicken filling:

300g (11oz) chicken mince

1 tablespoon coriander (cilantro) root, peeled and chopped

1 tablespoon ginger, peeled and chopped

2 tablespoons green shallot (spring onion, scallion), sliced

1 tablespoon fish sauce

½ tablespoon light soy sauce

½ tablespoon Chinese cooking wine

1 pinch white pepper, ground

1 tablespoon garlic, chopped

1 egg

Roll filling:

8 green prawns (shrimp) peeled and deveined

4 pieces of green shallot, white ends only, cut into 5cm (½ inch) strips

2 medium size carrots, cut into narrow strips

1 cup of shiitake mushrooms

Mix all chicken filling ingredients together and set aside in fridge to firm.

To make two rolls: Lay one bean curd skin on a clean, dry bench and cut into 10cm (4 inch) pieces.

Spoon the chicken mixture across the bottom edge of the bean curd skin. Lay half the prawns, sliced shiitake mushrooms, shallots and carrot on top of the chicken mixture. Roll up as you would a roulade or sushi roll.

Repeat this process with another bean curd skin to make a second roll.

Wrap tightly in glad wrap and squeeze out any excess air. Steam for 10 minutes or until firm and allow to cool. Fry the rolls in a deep fryer until the skins are golden brown and crispy. Remove and slice into 2.5cm (1 inch) wide pieces.

Serve with Cucumber Pickle (page 102.)

SERVES 4 AS AN ENTRÉE

Pandanus Chicken

The pandanus leaf is not eaten but is used to wrap the filling, imparting a distinctive grassy flavour.

MAKES 24 ROLLS

6 coriander (cilantro) roots, chopped
6 garlic cloves, chopped
2 tablespoons ginger, chopped
300 ml (10fl oz) sweet soy sauce
150 ml (5fl oz) black vinegar
1 tablespoon sesame oil
8 tablespoons soy sauce
2 tablespoons whiskey
500g (1lb) chicken thigh, diced 2.5cm (1 inch)
1 packet frozen pandanus leaves
4 tablespoons sesame seeds

Pound coriander (cilantro) root, garlic and ginger in a mortar and pestle. Mix with sweet soy, black vinegar, soy sauce, sesame oil and whiskey.

Set aside two thirds of the sauce. With the remaining one third of sauce, marinate chicken thigh pieces. Place single pandanus leaf on a clean surface and place one piece of marinated chicken about 2.5cm (1inch) from the bottom edge of the leaf. Fold the leaf over the chicken to form a triangle. Repeat this folding process up the leaf until 7.5cm (3 inch) from the top.

Take the loose end of the leaf and tuck back into the triangle to secure the bundle. Repeat with each piece of chicken.

Fry wrapped chicken pieces in vegetable oil in wok until chicken is cooked. Add sesame seeds to sauce and serve with cooked chicken bundles.

SERVES 6-8

Roast Chilli, Coconut & Peanut Chicken with Avocado Tamarind Salad

6 chicken breasts, skin on

Roasted Chilli, Coconut and Peanut Sauce:

75 ml (2½fl oz) vegetable oil

250 ml (8½fl oz) sweet chilli sauce

7 dried red chilli, roasted

100g (3½oz) shredded coconut, toasted

150g (5oz) peanuts, roasted

½ cup fried crispy shallot (spring onion, scallion)

¼ cup soy bean and chilli oil paste

1 tablespoon shrimp paste

1 tablespoon fish sauce

Tamarind Dressing:

125 ml (4¼fl oz) tamarind water

50 ml (1¾fl oz) lime juice

50g (1½oz) palm sugar

25 ml (¾fl oz) fish sauce

25 ml (¾fl oz) vegetable oil

Avocado Salad:

3 avocado, diced

3 tablespoons golden shallot, finely sliced

½ cup coriander (cilantro) leaves

2 red chilli, finely sliced

2 tablespoons peanuts, roasted and ground

Pawpaw (papaya) Sambal:

1 cup diced red pawpaw

1 tablespoon diced red onion

1 teaspoon finely diced ginger

1 tablespoon chopped coriander leaves

half tablespoon fish sauce

half tablespoon palm sugar

2 red chillies, finely diced

Seal chicken breast in a hot pan and place in 200°C (400°F, moderately hot, gas mark 5) oven to finish cooking—15 minutes.

Make the sauce: Blend all sauce ingredients until they form a smooth sauce.

Make the Tamarind Dressing: grind palm sugar in a mortar and pestle with lime juice, fish sauce and tamarind water. Once sugar has dissolved, slowly add the vegetable oil and set aside.

Make the Avocado Salad: mix avocado with red shallot, coriander (cilantro) leaves, chilli and toss the Tamarind Dressing.

Make the Pawpaw Sambal: dissolve palm sugar in fish sauce. Place all other sambal ingredients in a bowl and toss with palm sugar mixture.

To serve: Slice chicken on serving plates and spoon over the Roasted Chilli, Coconut and Peanut Sauce.

Serve with Avocado Salad and Pawpaw Sambal.

SERVES 6

Nonya Spatchcock with Pickled Lime & Chilli Jam

This recipe is an example of the Malay Nonya influence that is strongly reflected in the food of southern Thailand.

Nonya Paste:

4 red onions chopped

15 cloves garlic, peeled

3 tablespoons lemongrass, chopped

2 tablespoons ginger, peeled and chopped

5 tablespoons sambal olek

4 tablespoons fresh turmeric,
peeled and chopped

2 tablespoons roasted shrimp paste

4 x number 4-5 baby chickens, or 2kg chicken
pieces.

½ cup Nonya paste

Sauce:

2 tablespoons vegetable oil

1½ cups coconut milk

2 tablespoons tamarind water

1 teaspoon dark palm sugar

1 tablespoon fish sauce

Chilli Jam:

4 red capsicum (sweet pepper/bell pepper)

4 red onions

4 small chillies, chopped

1 cup (250ml, 8fl oz)vegetable oil

2 punnets cherry tomatoes

1 cup white sugar

1 cup (250ml, 8fl oz)fish sauce

2 tablespoons vegetable oil

1 pickled lime (see page 101)

4 teaspoons Chilli Jam

½ cup coriander (cilantro) sprigs

1 large red chilli, deseeded and cut into strips

To make the paste: place all ingredients in the bowl of a food processor and process to a paste.

Set aside. This paste will keep in the fridge for several weeks or can be frozen for up to 6 months.

Marinate the chicken: If using baby chickens split through the breastbone to open and then remove backbone and ribcage. Place chickens in a large bowl and coat with the Nonya paste. Set aside to marinate for several hours.

To make the sauce: fry 2-3 tablespoons of Nonya Paste gently in oil until fragrant, add the coconut milk, tamarind water, palm sugar and fish sauce. Bring to the boil and simmer for a few minutes for the flavours to come together. Taste and adjust with palm sugar and fish sauce if desired.

To make the Chilli Jam: cut the capsicum (sweet pepper/ bell pepper) and onion into 1cm (½ inch) dice. Heat the oil in a wok and fry the capsicum (sweet pepper/bell pepper), onion and chilli until very well browned. Add the tomatoes and simmer until the tomatoes have been reduced to a thick paste.

Add the sugar and fish sauce and simmer until jammy. Puree in a food processor. Transfer to clean container and refrigerate when cool—this keeps for several months in the refrigerator.

Preheat oven to 190°C (375°F, moderate, gas mark 4). The chicken can either be pan fried in a large heavy based frying pan and then finished off in the oven, or start on a barbecue then transfer to a tray and finish in the oven. The chicken will take about 20—25 minutes in the oven if using spatchcocks, or up to 40 minutes for large chicken pieces.

Heat oil in frying pan to moderate heat and place chicken pieces in skin side down, fry gently for 5 minutes and turn to other side and cook another 5 minutes. Transfer to tray and place in oven.

When cooked, divide chicken between serving plates and pour over the sauce. Garnish with pickled lime, chilli strips and a dollop of Chilli Jam. Finish with coriander.

Duck Fritters with Eggplant Pickle

Tasty duck morsels served with a delicious spicy pickle.

Eggplant Pickle:

1 large eggplant (aubergine) cut into 1.5cm slices and
lightly salted for 20 minutes
½ cup (125ml, 4fl oz)of peanut oil for frying
1 tablespoon red curry paste
4 tablespoons castor sugar
6 tablespoons rice vinegar
¼ cup chopped coriander (cilantro) leaves

Fritters:

½ barbecue Chinese duck
4 eggs
2 cups cooked coconut rice (see page 39)
2 green shallots (spring onion, scallion), finely sliced
¼ teaspoon five spice powder
salt and pepper
peanut oil for frying

To make the pickle: Pat the eggplant (aubergine) dry. Heat the oil until very hot and fry the eggplant (aubergine) slices until well browned on both sides. Remove to a bowl once they are cooked. When the last slice of eggplant (aubergine) has been removed from the oil, add the red paste and fry for one minute.

Add the sugar and vinegar to the paste and cook until it becomes syrupy. Pour over the eggplant (aubergine) and add the coriander (cilantro). Chop and stir well with a spoon to combine thoroughly and break up the eggplant (aubergine).

To make the fritters: Remove the duck flesh from the carcass and chop into small pieces. Whisk the egg in a bowl and stir in the rice, shallot (spring onion, scallion), five spice powder and duck. Season with the salt and pepper.

Heat the oil in a wok or frying pan and drop spoonfuls of fritter mix in and fry on both sides until browned.

Serve hot with the eggplant (aubergine) pickle.

SERVES 4 AS AN ENTRÉE

Cassia Smoked Duck Sausages Chargrilled with Wild Pepper Leaves

All over Thailand you will find stalls selling a variety of sausages. Some are made with fermented rice and smoked, some are grilled (broiled) or deep fried.

500g (1lb) duck mince
3 double Kaffir lime leaves, finely chopped
1 tablespoon fish sauce
¼ cup chopped garlic
1 teaspoon freshly ground white pepper
1 teaspoon roasted and ground coriander (cilantro) seed
½ teaspoon ground cinnamon
¼ cup coriander (cilantro) leaf and stem, chopped
1-2 tablespoons red curry paste.
sausage casings (available from gourmet butchers)
1 cup sawdust or woodchips
2 cups cassia bark, broken into pieces
1 cup brown sugar

To serve:
wild pepper leaves
butter lettuce
Sprigs of coriander (cilantro) and mint
finely chopped ginger
coarsely ground peanuts
finely chopped lime

To make the sausages: place the duck mince, lime leaves, fish sauce, garlic, pepper, coriander (cilantro) seeds, cinnamon, coriander (cilantro) leaves and curry paste into a food processor and process until well combined. Transfer to a bowl.

Spoon half the mixture into a piping bag and pipe into the sausage casings. Try and keep to uniform diameter of about 2.5cm. (1 inch). Tie off with kitchen string. Store in the fridge overnight to cure.

To smoke the sausages: Line a wok with 3 layers of aluminium foil and add the sawdust, cassia bark and sugar. Place a bamboo steamer basket over the wok. When the mixture starts to smoke, add the sausages. Cover and smoke until cooked, about 20-25 minutes.

Wrap the sausages in wild pepper leaves and char grill until heated through and the pepper leaves have softened. Transfer to serving plate. Make up a platter with lettuce and other garnishes.

The sausages are sliced and then wrapped in the lettuce with your selection of flavours.

Serve with a bowl of Chilli Lime Dipping Sauce (see index).

SERVES 4

Braised Duck in Chinese Star Anise Sauce

8 cups water

1 cup light soy sauce

1 cup (250ml, 8fl oz) shaoxing wine

½ cup yellow rock sugar

1 large knob ginger, peeled & sliced

4 cloves garlic, sliced

4 whole star anise

2 cinnamon sticks

2 pieces dried tangerine peel

8-12 duck Maryland
(thigh and leg pieces)

Bring all ingredients for the master stock to the boil, simmer on low heat for 1 hour. Strain and discard ingredients.

The stock will become intense in flavour over time, so just dilute with a little water. You can freeze the stock for later use or refrigerate. If refrigerating, you will need to bring the stock back to the boil once a week.

Preheat oven to 180°C (350°F, moderate, gas mark 4).

Trim duck pieces of excess fat and dry with paper towel. Place the pieces skin side down in a baking dish.

Heat the master stock to boiling in a saucepan and then pour over the duck pieces. Cover with aluminium foil and bake for 30 minutes. Turn over so the duck is skin side up. Cover again and place back in oven for 30 minutes.

Remove foil and cook another 30 minutes or until the skin has crisped up slightly.

Remove from oven and keep warm.

Strain master stock, transfer into saucepan and reduce down to sauce consistency.

Arrange the duck pieces on a large serving platter, pour sauce over.

Serve with wok seared Asian vegetables.

SERVES 4-6

Pork
[moo]

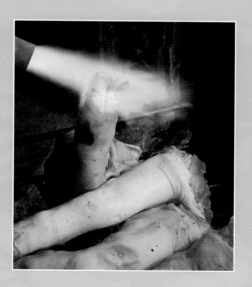

Pork Leg and Rice

The signage on the cart advertises three pork dishes—leg of pork with rice and fragrant mushroom, red pork and rice, plus crispy pork and rice.

Often served with special gravy, these stalls are identifiable by large pork hocks laying in a pot of simmering stock.

There is nothing complex about the dishes here. You buy a plate of rice and the pork of your choice with gravy ladled over it and some onion on the side.

Just point at the pork you want and hold up one finger for one dish. Or you can venture into Thai by saying: 'khaa moo' for leg of pork, 'moo daeng' for roasted red pork, while 'moo grob' is crispy pork … all are delicious.

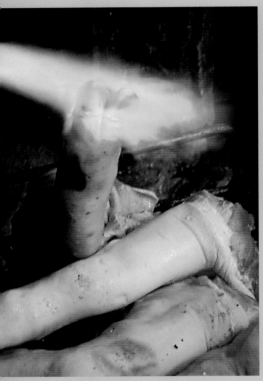

After the hairs are singed off pork hocks in the market, they are simmered in a master stock for hours.

Vendors who sell 'khaa moo' are easily identified by the hocks on display in their stalls. Very fatty but very delicious, the vendor serves a few slices of the pork on rice with a rich gravy.

Braised Pork Leg with Star Anise

This dish is found simmering in large cauldrons at markets all through Thailand. It's often served with hard boiled eggs and tofu that have been simmered in the same broth. Delicious served with steamed jasmine rice.

2 cups vegetable oil

1 leg of pork weighing about 1kg (2lb) from the chump end, or 2 pork hocks

2 litres water

4 cloves garlic

2 coriander (cilantro) roots, cleaned and scraped

½ teaspoon white peppercorns

2 tablespoons vegetable oil, extra

2 x 5cm (2 inch) pieces cassia bark

3 star anise

½ cup (125ml, 4fl oz) light soy sauce

¼ cup (60ml, 2fl oz) sweet soy sauce

¼ cup palm sugar

2 tablespoons fish sauce

1 x 2.5cm (1 inch) ginger, peeled and sliced

4 cloves garlic, unpeeled

4 boiled eggs, peeled (optional)

200g (6oz) firm tofu, cut into 2.5cm (1 inch) cubes (optional)

Heat the oil in a wok and carefully fry the pork until the skin is well coloured. Remove from oil and drain on paper towel.

Make a paste with the garlic, coriander (cilantro) roots and white peppercorns.

Heat the extra oil in a large pot and cook the garlic paste on a moderate heat until it is fragrant. Add the cassia bark, star anise, light and sweet soy, palm sugar, fish sauce, ginger and garlic. Bring to the boil and then add the pork. Simmer on a low heat until the meat is tender. This takes about 1 to 1½ hours. Remove the pork and set aside.

If using the tofu and eggs add to the stock and simmer a further 10 minutes.

Slice the pork and divide between serving bowls, portion the eggs and tofu if using, and ladle over some of the stock.

Serve with steamed jasmine rice.

SERVES 4-6

169

Braised Pork with Sweet Soy, Cinnamon, Star Anise & Ginger

The star anise in this recipe reflects the strong influence of the Chinese on Thai cuisine.

2 tablespoons vegetable oil

5 golden shallots, peeled and sliced

5 cloves garlic, peeled and chopped

650g (1lb 5oz) pork neck, cut into 2.5cm (1 inch) cubes

1 knob ginger, peeled and julienned

3 tablespoons sweet soy sauce (kecap manis)

2 tablespoons soy sauce

1 teaspoon ground white pepper

2 cups chicken stock

a few small red chillies, left whole

1 cinnamon stick

2 star anise

Heat oil in a wok. Add the shallot and garlic and sauté for 2 minutes over low heat.

Turn heat to high and add pork and cook until pork is sealed.

Add remaining ingredients and simmer over medium heat for about 45 minutes. When cooked there should be very little sauce left and the meat should have rich shiny glaze.

If it dries out too much during cooking add a little more chicken stock or water. When cooked transfer to serving plates, serve with jasmine rice and steamed vegetables.

SERVES 4

Stir Fried Chinese Broccoli with Marinated Pork

Marinated Pork:

500g (1lb) pork fillet
2 cloves garlic, minced
2 teaspoons ginger, minced
2 tablespoons light soy sauce
2 tablespoons dark soy sauce
4 tablespoons honey
2 tablespoons Chinese rice wine
1 teaspoon five spice powder
2 tablespoons Hoisin sauce

2 tablespoons vegetable oil
500g (1lb) Chinese broccoli or similar leafy green
4 cloves garlic, roughly chopped
2 green chillis, chopped
2 tablespoons water
2 tablespoons oyster sauce
1 tablespoon fish sauce
1 teaspoon white sugar
freshly ground white pepper

To make the marinade: Combine all marinating ingredients and marinade pork for 1-2 hours.

Place a cake rack into a roasting pan and partly fill with water, ensuring the water is below the rack.

Remove pork from marinade and place on rack.

Bake in a moderate oven (180°C, 350°F, gas mark 4) for 25- 30 minutes.

Brush well with left over marinade while the pork is roasting.

Cool and then slice thinly.

Heat oil to a moderate heat and fry the garlic until it is just starting to colour. Add the broccoli and stir-fry until the broccoli is wilted. Add the chillies, water, oyster sauce, fish sauce and sugar. Cook a minute or so further then toss through the pork and season with pepper.

SERVES 4

Chargrilled Pork Ribs with Citrus Soy Glaze & Pineapple Relish

Citrus and Soy Glaze:

1 large brown onion, roughly chopped

1 x 400g (14oz) tin of tomatoes

3 cloves garlic

½ cup (125ml, 4fl oz) white vinegar

4 tablespoons dark palm sugar

½ tablespoon salt

½ tablespoon freshly ground black pepper

2 tablespoons soy sauce

½ cup (125ml, 4fl oz) orange juice

Pineapple Relish:

1 fresh pineapple, cored and cut into small chunks

1 red capsicum (sweet pepper/bell pepper), diced

1 red chilli, deseeded and finely chopped

1 tablespoon finely chopped lemongrass

½ cup coriander (cilantro), chopped

1 tablespoon palm sugar

1 tablespoon fish sauce

2 tablespoons lime juice

4 sides baby pork back ribs, weighing about 750g (1½lb) each

2 tablespoons sweet soy sauce (kecap manis)

To make the glaze: place all the ingredients into a heavy based saucepan, bring to the boil and then reduce to a simmer for about 1 hour. Stir often as the glaze can stick. Cool and then transfer to the bowl of a blender and process to a smooth sauce. While the sauce is simmering toss the ribs with the sweet soy sauce and steam for 1 hour.

To make the relish: Mix together the pineapple, capsicum (sweet pepper/bell pepper), chilli, lemongrass and coriander (cilantro) in a bowl. In a separate bowl dissolve the sugar, fish sauce and lime juice. Add to the pineapple mix. Transfer to serving bowl.

To cook: put the ribs in a large bowl and toss with the sauce. Cook on a preheated barbecue turning often, until slightly charred. Serve with Pineapple Relish.

SERVES 6-8

Five Spice Pork
with Chinese Spiced Plum Sauce

Grown men have been known to cry when plums go out of season and this dish is removed from the Spirit House menu.

8 cups of Master Stock (see page 167)

Plum Sauce:

500g (1lb) light palm sugar

100 ml (3½fl oz) water

100 ml (3½fl oz) fish sauce

100 ml (3½fl oz) tamarind water (100g tamarind pulp dissolved in 100 ml warm water, then strained)

100g (¼oz) Hoisin sauce

10 whole plums, stone removed

Five Spice Pork:

1½kg (3lb) pork belly, skin on and bone removed

2 tablespoons Chinese five spice

2 tablespoons sea salt

1 tablespoon ground white pepper

butcher's twine

12 plum halves

2 bunches of bok choy or Asian green vegetables

To make the Plum Sauce: melt sugar in water in a heavy based pot until sugar starts to caramelise.

Add fish sauce, tamarind water, Hoisin sauce and plums and cook until plums are very soft and the sauce has a honey consistency. Strain.

To make the Five Spice Pork: Mix the five spice with salt and white pepper. Rub the inside (non skin side) of the pork with this mix. Roll the pork lengthways and tie tightly with butcher twine approx every 5cm (2 inches) along the pork. Bring master stock to boil. Place the pork in an ovenproof dish or pot.

Pour simmering master stock over the pork, making sure pork is completely covered. Cover the dish with baking paper and then foil to seal. Place in 160°C (325°F, moderately slow, gas mark 3) oven for 2½ hours. Remove pork from master stock and place on a tray to cool in fridge overnight. Cut pork into portions approx 250g (8oz) each.

To serve: Stir-fry the bok choy and portion on to individual serving plates.

Fry pork portions in deep fryer until gold and warm all the way through.

Slice pork. Arrange the pork slices on top of the stir fried green vegetables.

Pour over the plum sauce. Garnish with plum cheeks that have warmed in the sauce.

SERVES 6

Crispy Tofu Stuffed with Pork & Crab, with Sweet & Sour Ginger Lime Sauce

In Thailand, tofu is not used solely for vegetarians. Although silken tofu is difficult to handle, the end result is well worth the effort.

Sweet and Sour Ginger Lime Sauce:

225 ml (7½fl oz) coconut vinegar
375 grams (12oz) dark palm sugar
1½ cups of water
150 ml (5fl oz) light soy sauce
½ cup finely shredded ginger
½ cup (125ml, 4fl oz) lime juice

100g (3½oz) finely minced pork
liberal pinch of freshly ground white pepper
1 teaspoon chopped garlic
2 green shallot (spring onion, scallion) finely chopped
¼ cup chopped coriander (cilantro) leaves
½ tablespoon soy sauce
½ tablespoon oyster sauce
1 teaspoons sugar
1 teaspoon sesame oil
50g (1¾oz) crab meat
1 packet Japanese silken firm tofu, approx 400g (14oz)
plain flour
2 egg whites, beaten until frothy
2 cups vegetable oil
extra green shallot (spring onion, scallion) and coriander (cilantro) leaves for garnish

To make the sauce: combine all ingredients except lime juice in a saucepan and bring to the boil, cook uncovered for about 10 minutes. Mix should be reduced by about half. Stir in lime juice off the heat.

Put pork, pepper, garlic, green shallot (spring onion, scallion), coriander (cilantro) leaves, oyster sauce, soy sauce, sugar, and sesame oil into food processor and process to a sticky paste. Mix in the crab meat.

Cut the silken tofu into half lengthways and shape pork mix into equal shapes, place on the tofu and top with the remaining tofu. Place on heatproof plate. Refrigerate for 1 hour and then steam for about 20-25 minutes. Chill in refrigerator for a minimum of 2 hours.

Cut bean curd into 6 pieces, roll in flour and then into egg white.

Heat oil in a wok to medium and deep fry tofu until golden brown—takes about 7-10 minutes. Drain on absorbent kitchen paper.

Transfer to serving plate and garnish with green shallot (spring onion, scallion) and coriander (cilantro) leaves. Serve with Sweet and Sour Ginger and Lime Sauce.

SERVES 6

While poultry and pork are the most commonly used meats in all Asian cuisines, beef is also cooked in Thailand, but less frequently as it is expensive to buy. There are some classic Thai beef dishes, the most well known probably being Thai Rare Beef Salad with its fiery dressing, variations of which are found from the south to the north of Thailand.

Massaman Beef Curry, a mild curry influenced by Muslim traders in southern Thailand, is spiced with cardamom, cloves and cinnamon. As it is used for hearty stew-like dishes, beef is an ideal meat to use, and is one of the most fragrant Thai curries.

To tenderise beef, it is often slowly braised in a Chinese master stock or marinated in hot spicy dressings that also increase the flavour. Out on the streets, vendors add thin slices of beef to a range of soups, noodles and stir-fry.

Beef
[Nua]

Ice

Late at night, large trucks drop huge blocks of ice to small shop/houses that turn the blocks of ice into shaved ice. The shaved ice is then put into sacks and delivered in some amazing homemade carriages to shops and vendors in the local area.

Ice keeps Bangkok fresh. All day long, these bizarre rickshaw style vehicles deliver ice to markets and street food stalls, ensuring that raw ingredients stay fresh.

This thriving industry in ice production and delivery makes eating street food in Bangkok much safer than some other Asian countries. On our Tag-Along tours, we choose vendors who store their ingredients on ice and only eat freshly cooked food—none of our tour group has ever been sick.

With no electricity on the street to power refrigerators, dessert vendors ladle their concoctions over a bowl of shaved ice to create an instantly cool and refreshingly tasty treat.

Drink vendors will store their drinks on ice, but if you want a drink to carry around with you, they will simply put ice in a plastic bag, pour in the drink, add a straw and tie it up with a rubber band. The rubber band replaces the cup holder, plus it acts like a shock absorber ensuring the drink doesn't spill when riding your motorbike.

Issan Style Barbecue Beef with Wild Pepper Leaves

The wild pepper leaves used in this recipe impart a subtle aniseed flavour when cooked. If unavailable, substitute with banana leaves.

Hot and Sour Sauce:

1 fresh red chilli

1 clove garlic

2 teaspoons sugar

1 tablespoon rice vinegar

4 tablespoons lime juice

3 tablespoons fish sauce

500g (1lb) lean beef mince

1 tablespoon vegetable oil

2 tablespoons finely chopped lemongrass

2 tablespoons finely chopped golden shallot or brown onion

4 cloves finely chopped garlic

2 tablespoons fish sauce

3 teaspoons white sugar

1 teaspoon five spice powder

½ teaspoon freshly ground white pepper

¼ teaspoon powdered turmeric

30 wild pepper leaves

bamboo skewers

vegetable oil, extra

1 butter lettuce

sprigs of mint, basil and coriander (cilantro)

To make the sauce: pound the chilli and garlic to a fine paste in mortar, blend in sugar, slowly stir in the vinegar, lime juice and fish sauce. Place in a serving bowl.

In a bowl combine beef, oil, lemongrass, shallot, garlic, fish sauce, sugar, five spice powder, pepper and turmeric. Mix well, marinate refrigerated for 2 hours or overnight.

Place a generous tablespoon of meat onto a pepper leaf and roll into a log shape, leaving the ends open. Repeat until all the meat is used. Thread horizontally onto bamboo skewers, brush with extra oil.

Preheat barbecue to moderate and grill skewers until cooked—about 5 minutes on each side.

Wash the lettuce leaves whole and arrange with the herbs on a platter with a bowl of Hot and Sour Sauce and the cooked meat skewers. To eat, put the roll on to a lettuce leaf with some of the fresh herbs. Roll up and dip into the sauce and eat out of your hand.

SERVES 8

Stir-Fried Beef with Roasted Chilli Paste & Thai Basil

1 teaspoon coriander seeds

1 teaspoon cumin seed

1 tablespoon fish sauce

250g (8oz) rump steak, cut into stir-fry strips

1-2 tablespoons vegetable oil

1 tablespoon roasted chilli paste

1 tablespoon oyster sauce

1 tablespoon fish sauce, extra

pinch of sugar to taste

1 bunch broccolini, cut into florets

½ cup Thai basil leaves

3 tablespoons fried golden shallot

generous pinch of white pepper

generous pinch roasted chilli powder

coriander (cilantro) leaves to garnish

Roast coriander and cumin seeds over a low heat in a heavy based frying pan until fragrant. Grind to a powder and toss with the beef and fish sauce. Marinate for an hour.

Heat oil in a wok and stir-fry the beef until cooked as preferred—about 2-3 minutes for medium rare.

Turn down the heat to moderate and add chilli paste, oyster sauce, fish sauce and sugar and a little water if necessary.

Then add the broccolini and basil leaves. Stir-fry until just cooked for around a minute or so.

Then add the fried golden shallot, white pepper and chilli powder.

Transfer to serving plate and sprinkle with coriander (cilantro) leaves.

SERVES 4

Chargrilled Beef & Eggplant with Chilli & Basil

*Use apple eggplant (aubergine) if available—
they taste like a green bean and are often eaten raw.*

Dressing:

1 tablespoon chilli paste

⅓ cup lime juice

1 tablespoons palm sugar

1 tablespoons fish sauce

2-4 small red chillies, finely chopped

1 eggplant (aubergine), cut into quarters, lengthways

2 tablespoons vegetable oil

500g (1lb) eye fillet, in 2-3 pieces

1 punnet of cherry tomatoes

2 green shallot (spring onion, scallion), thinly sliced

1 cup of mixed coriander (cilantro), mint and basil leaves

generous pinch of roasted chilli powder

4 tablespoons crispy shallot

To make the dressing: Combine all the dressing ingredients in a mixing bowl and stir until sugar is dissolved.

Toss eggplant (aubergine) in 1 tablespoon of the vegetable oil and cook on a moderate barbecue, turning often until soft. This takes about 10-15 minutes. Remove and when cool cut into 2.5cm (1 inch) slices.

Heat barbecue to high, add remaining oil and sear beef on one side for 2-3 minutes.

Turn and cook for 2-3 minutes more. The beef should be rare to medium, cook further if desired.

Remove from heat and rest, lightly covered with foil for 10-15 minutes.

Cut beef into thin slices and place in a large mixing bowl with the eggplant (aubergine) and remaining ingredients.

Add dressing and toss to coat, then transfer to a serving plate.

Lemongrass Marinated Beef with Green Mango Salad & Tamarind

Beef marinade:

1 stalk of lemongrass, bottom half, bruised and chopped

1 large red chilli, chopped

2 coriander (cilantro) roots, cleaned and scrapped

2 Kaffir lime leaves, finely chopped

zest of 1 lime

1 tablespoon galangal, peeled and chopped

1 tablespoon ginger, peeled and chopped

1 teaspoon sesame oil

1 tablespoon vegetable oil

1 teaspoon sugar

1 teaspoon fish sauce

500 grams (1lb) eye fillet or other good quality beef

Tamarind Dressing:

1 clove garlic

1 large chilli, chopped

1 tablespoons light palm sugar

1 tablespoon fish sauce

2 tablespoons lime juice

2 tablespoons tamarind water

Green Mango Salad:

1 green mango, cut into julienne
(or green pawpaw/papaya)

1 ripe mango, cut into julienne

1 cup of mixed mint, coriander (cilantro) and basil

2 cups of watercress sprigs

2 sliced golden shallots

tamarind dressing

2 tablespoons crispy golden shallots to garnish

To make the marinade: place the lemongrass, chilli, coriander (cilantro) roots, Kaffir lime leaves, lime zest, galangal and ginger in mortar and pestle and pound to a paste. Transfer to a bowl and mix in the remaining ingredients. Add the beef and coat well and then place in refrigerator for minimum of 2 hours or overnight.

To make the Tamarind Dressing: in a mortar and pestle make a paste with the garlic and chilli. Transfer to a mixing bowl and add remaining ingredients, stirring to dissolve the sugar.

To cook the beef: preheat oven to 220°C (450°F, moderately hot, gas mark 5). Heat a heavy based frying pan with 1 tablespoon of vegetable oil until the oil starts to smoke.

Drain meat from the marinade and add to pan, searing well for several minutes on all sides.

Transfer to a baking dish and place in oven. Cook for 12-15 minutes for medium rare.

Remove from oven and rest, lightly covered with aluminium foil for 15 minutes. Then slice thinly.

To make the Mango Salad: Combine all the salad ingredients except the crispy shallot in a large mixing bowl and toss gently to coat with the dressing.

Transfer to a serving platter or 4 individual entrée plates and then place the sliced beef on top of the salad. Finish with the crispy shallots.

SERVES 4 AS AN ENTRÉE

Sweets
[Khanom]

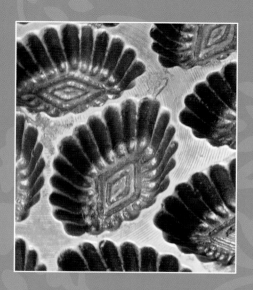

Many Thai desserts on the menu in restaurants are available for a fraction of the price on the street outside. After you've finished your main course, pay the bill and head out to the street for desserts. You can find mango and sticky rice, tup tim grob and a myriad of coconut and syrup based fruit and agar agar desserts at the various vendor stalls.

The Lanna Thai

A great way to spend an evening is to take the BTS sky train on the On Nut line to Thong Lor station to have dinner at the fabulous Face Bar which is home to Lanna Thai restaurant.

After exiting Thong Lor station, walk down Soi 38 passing a great collection of dessert stalls and food vendors as you stroll. About 100 metres down the soi on the left hand side is Face Bar, which is set in three beautiful Thai style houses. You come for the food but you stay for the setting ... it is amazing.

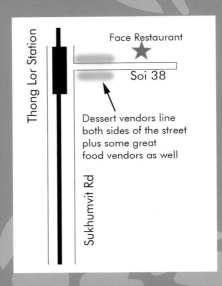

Thong Lor Station

Face Restaurant

★

Soi 38

Dessert vendors line both sides of the street plus some great food vendors as well

Sukhumvit Rd

Persian Fairy Floss

Ayuddhaya is a fascinating town about 70 km north of Bangkok. Around the 16th century it was the Thai capital and a thriving port with trading posts established by merchants from Arabia, China, Japan, Portugal and England. Ayuddhaya was the original Venice of the East with elaborate temples, gilded Buddha's and ornate palaces all connected by canals. It was one of the largest cities in the world at the time, presided over by the Thai royal family. The Burmese army sacked the city in 1767 ending a golden era that stretched back 400 years.

Our Tag-Along tour goes to Ayuddhaya to explore the ruins and, more importantly, to learn the secrets of making 'roti sai mai'—silken threads of jerked sugar that are often called Persian fairy floss. This is a specialty food rarely found outside of Ayuddhaya and was probably introduced to the area by the old Arab traders.

Sai Mai is easy to find—hundreds of stalls line the streets around the town, making or selling bags of fairy floss and wafer thin 'roti' or bread which is used to wrap the strands of fairy floss, rather similar to a sugar sandwich. Fairy floss comes in different colours and flavours.

Making the fairy floss looks deceptively easy. Sugar and water is boiled until caramelised, then cooled into a toffee. An oil/flour roux is spread on the table.

The toffee is stretched into a circle that is then stretched, turned back on itself and stretched again. This whole process is repeated over and over until the sugar starts to get a hair-like texture. The roux prevents the strands from sticking. It is very strenuous work.

Once the right texture has been achieved, the fairy floss is portioned out and put in bags.

A lightning knife

A street vendor extrudes long strands of dough on a chopping board and with lightning-fast speed chops even-sized pieces that are deep fried into small round donuts.

Tup tim grob

The bowl of red mystery balls on the left end of this stall make up a delicious dessert called 'tup tim grob'. Water chestnuts are coated in tapioca flour that has red dye added, boiled and then served with coconut milk flavoured with pandanus, sugar syrup and ice—as are most of the other various multi-coloured noodles and gelatinous treats. The pickled fruits are often served with sweet ginger tea syrup over ice. In short, there is a huge variety of desserts on offer and sometimes the best thing is simply to do a 'dessert Russian roulette'—shut your eyes, point at a few things and take your chances—yum!

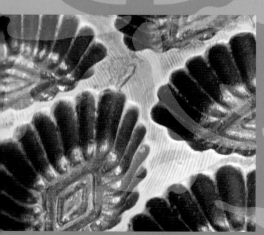

Cake moulds

Heavy brass dessert moulds are found in Chinatown. These moulds come in a range of sizes and are designed to sit on top of charcoal stoves.

The weight of the brass helps to evenly distribute the heat, while the intricate patterns create pleasingly shaped sweet cakes.

Sweet cakes cooked in cake moulds

Spice Fruit Sorbets with Coconut Wafer

Sugar Syrup:

250g (8½oz) caster sugar

250 ml (8½fl oz) water

Watermelon and Star Anise Sorbet:

500 ml (17fl oz) watermelon juice, strained

250 ml (8½fl oz) sugar syrup

½ tablespoon sambuca, or a star anise based liqueur

1 tablespoon lemon juice

Lychee and Ginger Sorbet:

2 cans lychees, strained

250 ml (8½fl oz) sugar syrup

1 tablespoon grated ginger

2 tablespoons reisling wine

½ tablespoon lime juice

Banana and Passionfruit Sorbet:

200g (7oz) peeled bananas

250 ml (8½fl oz) passionfruit juice

215 ml (7½fl oz) water

2 tablespoons glucose syrup

150g (5oz) castor sugar

1 tablespoon orange juice

Coconut Wafers:

120g (4oz) butter

100g (3½oz) glucose

100g (3½oz) plain flour

180g (6oz) sugar

½ teaspoon ground ginger

¼ cup shredded coconut

To make the sugar syrup: Bring caster sugar and water gently to simmer until the sugar dissolves, then cool in refrigerator over night. Then make sorbet as per instructions below.

For each sorbet:

Combine all ingredients in a food processor and blend until smooth then strain if needed. Churn in an ice-cream machine if available or pour into a container and freezer for several hours. Remove from the freezer and whip, then freeze again for a further 2 hours. Let the mixture stand for 5 minutes to soften slightly before serving.

To make the wafers: melt butter and glucose in a double boiler. Combine flour, sugar, ginger and coconut in a separate bowl and pour over the butter and glucose mixture, stirring until it forms a paste. Place mixture into the fridge and allow to set. Remove mixture from the fridge when it has hardened and roll into small marble-like balls. Place on greaseproof paper, allowing room between each ball as mixture will spread when cooking. Place into a 145°C (300°F, slow, gas mark 2) pre-heated oven and cook for 12 minutes until golden. Remove and place on a hard surface to cool. Serve with scooped sorbet.

SERVES 4-6

Coconut Slice

Delicious sweet taste served with coffee.

5 eggs
300g (11oz) caster sugar
400 ml (14fl oz) cream
180g (6oz) desiccated coconut

Whisk eggs and sugar until a pale colour. Add cream and coconut and combine mixture to a thin paste. Place mixture into a lined baking dish and cook in a bain-marie in a 160°C (300°F, slow, gas mark 2) pre-heated oven for 1½ hours. Allow to cool. Refrigerate overnight before cutting into preferred slices or squares.

Fresh Fruit with Coconut Cream

2 cups coconut cream
1 pandanus leaf
2 teaspoons rice flour, mixed with a little of the coconut cream to form a paste
¼ teaspoon salt
¾ cup white sugar
800g (28oz) fresh tropical fruit—pawpaw (papaya), mangoes, lychees, melons—peeled and sliced
1 tablespoon toasted sesame seeds
mint sprigs to garnish

Heat the coconut cream with the pandanus leaf. Stir in the rice flour paste and salt and simmer until thick, about 10 minutes.

Add sugar and stir until dissolved. Remove the pandanus leaf and chill in the refrigerator.

Serve over the fruit and garnish with the sesame seeds and mint.

SERVES 4-6

Chocolate Tart with Star Anise Anglaise

A bitter-sweet chocolate tart.

ONE TART MAKES 12 SLICES

Tart Pastry:

250g (8oz) unsalted butter, cubed

2 tablespoons sugar

400g (14oz) plain flour

4 tablespoons cocoa powder

4 egg yolks

3 tablespoons cold water

Tart Filling:

300 ml (10fl oz) cream

300g (11oz) dark chocolate, chopped

1 tablespoon brandy

2 egg yolks

Star Anise Anglaise:

250 ml (8½fl oz) milk

3 star anise

125 ml (4¼fl oz) cream

4 egg yolks

120g (4oz) caster sugar

2 tablespoons cocoa powder

1½ cups double cream

To make the pastry: place butter and sugar into a bowl and using fingertips, mix until bread crumb consistency. Add egg yolks, flour and cocoa powder and stir mixture until a dough forms, adding water if necessary. Wrap dough in plastic film and refrigerate for 30 minutes before using. Roll out pastry and place into a greased 12 inch flan tin. Cover with baking paper and blind bake for 20 minutes in 180C oven. Remove paper and bake for a further 10 minutes. Cool tart shell.

Make the filling: bring cream to a simmer. Remove cream from heat and add the chopped chocolate whisking until it melts. Cool at room temperature stirring occasionally. When cool, whisk in egg yolks and brandy and strain into cooked tart shell. Refrigerate until set.

Make the Star Anise Anglaise: Place milk, star anise and cream into a pot and bring to a simmer. Remove from heat and cool slightly. Whisk egg yolks and sugar in a large bowl and add milk mixture a little at a time, whisking continuously. Place mixture in a clean pot and cook on a low heat, stirring constantly with a wooden spoon until the mixture thickens and coats the back of the spoon. Strain and allow to cool in the fridge.

Dust the chocolate tart with cocoa powder and cut into slices. Serve with star anise anglaise and double cream.

Mung Bean Dumplings with Ginger & Cinnamon Broth

60g (1¾oz) dried mung beans

1 tablespoon sugar

pinch of salt

100g (3½oz) glutinous rice flour

⅓ cup warm water

540g (1lb, 1oz) chopped palm sugar

6 cinnamon sticks

40g (1oz) fresh sliced ginger

1.25 litres (2 pints) water

8 cinnamon sticks, to garnish

2 teaspoons roasted sesame seeds, to serve

Soak mung beans in cold water for 1 hour, then drain. Place in a saucepan of water, bring to boil then reduce heat and simmer for 20-25 minutes or until beans are tender. Drain well. Place in a bowl with sugar and salt and mash well, allow to cool. Roll mixture into twelve even sized balls.

Combine flour and warm water and mix to a soft but firm dough. Knead well on a floured surface. Shape into twelve balls. Roll each ball into a 6cm (2½ inch) disk and wrap around mung bean balls. Seal dough by pinching together. Shake off any excess flour.

Boil a large pot of water. Carefully drop a few dumplings at a time into the water. Cook for 2-3 minutes or until balls float to the surface. Remove balls from water and rinse under cold water. Drain well and set aside.

Combine the palm sugar, cinnamon and ginger and 1.25 litres (2 pints) of water in a medium saucepan, stir over heat until sugar dissolves. Bring to the boil then reduce heat and simmer for 20 minutes.

Add dumplings and cook for a further ten minutes.

Serve dumplings in bowls with broth, ginger and garnish with cinnamon sticks and sprinkle with sesame seeds.

SERVES 4

Tropical Fruit
Spring Rolls with Palm Sugar & Ginger Sauce

A spring roll with a difference.

Palm Sugar and Ginger Sauce:

200g (7oz) light palm sugar

2 tablespoons finely sliced ginger

30 ml (1fl oz) water

small squeeze lime juice

2 bananas

1 pineapple

1 rockmelon

8 lychees, peeled and cut in halves

1 packet of 24cm (10-inch) spring roll wrappers

several sprigs mint leaves

1 beaten egg

cinnamon sugar

To make the sauce: bring palm sugar and water to simmer. Add ginger and remove from heat. Allow to cool, add lime juice to cut the sweetness.

Cut bananas, pineapple and rockmelon into 7.5cm (3inch) pieces.

Place thawed spring roll wrapper on the bench. Position fruit and mint leaves in centre of wrapper and roll as you would a normal spring roll. Brush a small amount of the beaten egg on final edge of wrapper to seal.

Deep fry rolls in clean vegetable oil.

Remove from fryer and lightly dust with cinnamon sugar.

Cut on the diagonal and serve with ice cream. Drizzle sauce over sugar rolls.

SERVES 8

Chilled Watermelon & Lychee Parfait with Lime & Vodka Syrup

A refreshing summer dessert that's easy to prepare.

zest and juice of 2 limes
½ cup white sugar
90 ml (3fl oz) of vodka
3 cups diced watermelon
3 cups deseeded lychees, (tinned are fine if lychees out of season)
2 tablespoons diced candied ginger
lime or lemon sorbet (other tropical flavours like mango are also delicious)

Combine lime juice, zest and sugar in a saucepan over a moderate heat. Stir only until the sugar is dissolved, bring to the boil and then simmer for 5 minutes. Remove from heat and cool, stir in the vodka.

Any unused syrup will keep for months in the fridge.

Take 6 parfait glasses—Pilsener beer glasses make a great presentation—and layer the watermelon, lychees and ginger into parfait glasses. Top with a scoop of sorbet then drizzle with vodka syrup.

SERVES 4-6

Lemon Grass Panacotta with Red Papaya & Candied Ginger Tuille

300 ml (10fl oz) cream
100 ml (3½fl oz) milk
100g (3½oz) lemongrass
95g caster sugar
2 gelatine leaves

Candied Ginger and Rice Tuille:
25g (1oz) rice flour
25g (1oz) plain four
50g (2½oz) icing sugar
25g (1oz) butter
50g (2½oz) egg whites
20g (1oz) candied ginger, chopped fine

Red Papaya Salad:
50g (2½oz) caster sugar
50 ml (1¾fl oz) water
1 stalk of lemongrass
1 small red papaya, diced
1 tablespoon mint, finely sliced

Bring milk, cream, sugar and lemongrass to a simmer. Remove the mixture from the heat and allow the lemongrass to infuse—about 1 hour. In a separate bowl, soak the gelatine leaves in a small amount of warm water. Then squeeze the leaves lightly to remove excess water. Strain the lemongrass mixture and add the soaked gelatine leaves. Stir until leaves have dissolved. Pour into four individual dessert moulds and refrigerate overnight.

To make the Tuille: mix all ingredients together and place in fridge to set. Spread onto greaseproof paper and bake at 135°C (275°F, gas mark 1, cool) for 13 minutes. Remove from greaseproof paper while still hot. It will be quite pliable and can be left flat or moulded over a rolling pin into a curved shape for presentation. Allow to cool, store in airtight container.

To make the Red Papaya Salad: dissolve caster sugar in water, bring to the boil and infuse with lemongrass to make sugar syrup. Allow to cool. Mix sugar syrup with diced papaya and mint.

To serve, unmould each panacotta onto individual serving plate, spoon on a little diced red papaya salad and top with a piece of Ginger Tuille.

SERVES 4

Coconut Custard with Jackfruit

One of the best known Thai desserts, coconut custards are often served as a topping for sticky rice or sometimes steamed inside small squash. This version uses fresh jackfruit, which may be difficult to find—the tinned fruit will also produce excellent results.

1½ cups (400ml) coconut milk

3 large eggs

2 egg yolks

1 cup light palm sugar

2 teaspoons cornflour, dissolved in a little water

200g (6oz) jackfruit flesh, roughly chopped

Whisk together the coconut milk, eggs, egg yolks, palm sugar and cornflour. Divide the jackfruit between heatproof ramekins. Pour over the custard. Place ramekins in a bamboo steamer and place steamer over a wok with boiling water. Steam for about 30 minutes until the custard is set. Cool before serving.

SERVES 4-6

Clam Shell Delight

The dumplings are supposed to resemble clams floating in a sea of coconut milk—very poetic!

1½ cups rice flour
¾ cup tapioca starch
1 cup (250ml, 8fl oz) hot water
3 cups (750ml, 24fl oz) coconut milk
1 cup light palm sugar
1 teaspoon salt
2 tablespoons toasted sesame seeds, to serve

Combine the rice flour with ½ cup of the tapioca starch in a bowl. Add the hot water and mix to make pliable dough. Knead until smooth.

Dust hands with left over tapioca starch and pinch dough into 1cm (½ inch) balls. Roll into dumplings and dust with tapioca starch.

Bring a large pot of water to boil and add the dumplings in batches. Stir to avoid sticking and cook until they rise to the surface. Remove with a slotted spoon and set aside.

Combine the coconut milk, palm sugar and salt in a saucepan. Bring to the boil and simmer for a few minutes. Drop in the dumplings and heat through. Divide between serving bowls and sprinkle with toasted sesame seeds.

SERVES 4-6

Tup Tim Grob

A light and refreshing dessert that is typical of the Thai combination of textures that can taste very foreign to the Western palate. The name translates as 'rubies' and many versions of this type of sweet can be found all over South East Asia. Unlike in the West, Asian cooks are not afraid of a bit of vivid food colouring!

250g (8oz) tinned water chestnuts
1 cup (250ml, 8 fl oz) water tinted with a few drops of red food colouring
½ cup tapioca starch
1 cup white sugar
1 cup (250ml, 8fl oz) water
pinch of salt
½ cup (125ml, 4fl oz) coconut cream
1 cup crushed ice

Roughly chop the water chestnuts and place in the coloured water. Allow to soak for 30 minutes, then drain and set aside.

Bring a large pot of water to boil. Roll the water chestnuts in the tapioca starch and poach in the boiling water until they float to the surface. Remove with a slotted spoon and drop into a bowl of cold water.

Dissolve the sugar in the water and bring to boil. Remove from heat and allow to cool completely.

Mix the salt into the coconut cream.

When ready to serve, drain the water chestnuts and divide between serving bowls. Then divide the sugar syrup and crushed ice between the bowls. Spoon over the coconut cream and serve.

SERVES 4-6

Index